Making Scripture Memory Fun

Loveland, Colorado

MAKING SCRIPTURE MEMORY FUN

Credits

Contributors: Lisa Flinn, Nanette Goings, Mikal Keefer, Dan Nehrbass, Lori Haynes Niles, Liz Shockey, Jennifer Wilger, and Barbara Younger.
Editor: Beth Rowland Wolf
Quality Control Editor: Jody Brolsma
Chief Creative Officer: Joani Schultz
Copy Editor: Helen Turnbull
Designer and Art Director: Jean Bruns
Cover Art Director: Jeff A. Storm
Cover Designer: Becky Hawley
Computer Graphic Artist: Theresa Mesa
Cover Illustrator: Tammy Smith
Illustrator: Susan Nethery
Production Manager: Peggy Naylor

Library of Congress Cataloging-in-Publication Data

Making Scripture memory fun.
       p.   cm.
  Includes indexes.
  ISBN 0-7644-2065-8
    1. Bible--Memorizing.   2. Christian education of children.
  I. Group Publishing.
  BS617.7.M35   1998
  268'.432--dc21   98-14148
                                                  CIP

10 9 8 7 6 5 4 3   07 06 05 04 03 02 01 00
Printed in the United States of America.
Visit our Web site: www.grouppublishing.com

ontents

Verse	Title	

Introduction

As Christians, we share a passionate love and a high regard for God's Word. We gather regularly to listen to sermons that explain Bible principles. We recognize the value of spending time in personal study of Scripture to better know and follow God. We make great efforts to teach God's Word to our children. And we memorize Scripture—hiding it in our hearts—to deepen our understanding and our faith.

But for many of us, and especially for children, memorization is the most dreaded part of Bible study. While none of us would doubt the value of being so familiar with the Bible that we can quote from it, many Christians aren't so sure about the value of the methods traditionally used to memorize Scripture. To many, Scripture memory seems boring—a meaningless, ineffective, rote process that turns people, especially children, away from the church and away from God.

In too many cases, Bible memory work becomes a competition between children, a divisive force that creates enemies ready to one-up each other instead of the encouraging, loving, tightknit body God wants. In too many churches, Bible memory becomes a test for children, who must prove they can recite a verse perfectly before they're allowed to participate in the fun. And too often memorizing God's Word becomes not a way to know and love God, but a way to obtain a prize whether it be a toy, a shiny ribbon, or a new Bible.

None of these experiences foster a deep love for Scripture or an understanding of God. And most of the time, these "learning" experiences don't even give the results they were intended for. While children may memorize a verse, they don't understand what the verse means and they can't apply it to their lives. Plus, very few children remember their memory verse for extended periods of time. In fact, most children would be hard-pressed to remember even two or three of all the verses they've been asked to memorize in their entire lives.

Wouldn't it be great if there was a way to help children memorize Scripture that was more effective, more fun, and more lasting? Wouldn't it be great if children could memorize God's Word without fear and competition? And wouldn't it be great if children memorized Scripture because it was relevant and meaningful—because they *wanted* to learn God's Word?

Making Scripture Memory Fun will help you help children to know, understand and memorize eighty key Scripture verses. This new resource is effective because it approaches Scripture memory in a new way.

Each memory activity in *Making Scripture Memory Fun* seeks first to explain the verse to children in a way that's thought-provoking and life-relevant. The children don't just learn the words of the verse. They learn what it means and they learn how to apply it to their lives. Throughout each activity, the children are working with and repeating the words of the verse so that by the time the activity is over, the children are so familiar with the verse they have memorized it.

Making Scripture Memory Fun also seeks to help all kinds of learners make intellectual connections with Scripture. This book uses memory techniques that capitalize on an individual child's intellectual "frame of mind." This frame of mind refers to a child's natural intellectual skill. We all know people who are "natural athletes" and people who seem to have been born with unusually strong musical skills. We might explain those abilities as talents or gifts. But according to Howard Gardner, a professor of education at Harvard University, these abilities are more accurately called "frames of mind" or "intelligences."

According to Gardner, there are at least eight basic intelligences: linguistic intelligence, logical-mathematical intelligence, musical intelligence, interpersonal intelligence, reflective intelligence, kinesthetic intelligence, visual-spatial intelligence, and naturalistic intelligence. Gardner says that everyone has all eight intelligences in varying degrees. And he also says that children learn better when they're taught through activities that cause them to use their preferred intelligence. For example, the natural athlete will more easily learn when she can use body skills to help reinforce the material, and a musical child will find learning easier when he can use music as a tool.

Making Scripture Memory Fun has adapted Gardner's theory to help make Scripture memory easier and fun. When children learn according to their intelligence, they're more interested in what is being taught. They'll also learn more and retain more of what they learn. In this book, you'll find that each activity is geared to a specific intelligence. Read the descriptions of each intelligence listed below and think about the children in your class who have each of these intelligences. Choose activities that will appeal to the kinds of learners you have in your classroom. By using a variety of activities you'll be sure to have something that strikes a chord with every child in your class. Here are the eight intelligences:

Linguistic Intelligence

Linguistic intelligence is the ability to understand and use language as a learning tool. Children who have this intelligence may like to read or write, but they may also like to give debate or speeches. They enjoy the meanings of words and the find satisfaction in expressing themselves through language.

Logical-Mathematical Intelligence

People with a strong sense of logical-mathematical intelligence understand cause-and-effect relationships. They want to know how things work and they ask a lot of questions. They enjoy logical outcomes and derive satisfaction from numbers and equations.

Musical Intelligence

Musical people find meaning and will seek to express themselves in the patterns, tones, and rhythms of music. Some people with a strong musical intelligence are performers of music. Some are composers of music. And some find great meaning in simply listening to music.

Interpersonal Intelligence

Interpersonal people are social people. They understand and empathize with people. They're comfortable in both large and small social settings. They're great discussers, and they find great significance in activities that allow them to interact with others.

Reflective Intelligence

People with a strong sense of reflective (or intrapersonal) intelligence are grounded in a profound sense of self-understanding. These people are independent and like to work alone. They're introspective and enjoy getting in touch with themselves and understanding their own motives.

Bodily-Kinesthetic Intelligence

Bodily-kinesthetic intelligence refers to the ability to use body skills to solve problems or as a means of self-expression. People who are strong in this intelligence enjoy pursuits such as sports, dancing, crafts, and acting. They like to touch things and gain meaning from various textures. You may find that children with this intelligence fidget or move around a lot in class.

Visual-Spatial Intelligence

This is the ability to understand space relationships. They're good at manipulating space the way an architect does. People with a strong visual-spatial intelligence have a good sense of direction—they're natural navigators. And they express themselves well in visual arts such as painting or film. These people need to see things to understand them.

Naturalistic Intelligence

People with this intelligence have the ability to recognize patterns in nature. They easily understand the differences between various plants or animals. These people may collect rocks or plants or bugs and may organize them according to their similarities or differences. These people enjoy any activity that allows them to explore the natural world.

Scripture is one of God's best gifts to us. It is God's revelation of himself to his people and the world. It is the authority that defines our faith in terms of what we think about God and creation and also how we behave in relationship to God and others. In the Bible we find comfort and hope, challenge and admonition. As teachers of children in the church, you've been given an exciting and sacred task—to encourage children to love God and cherish his Word. Scripture itself encourages us to use every opportunity and every method available to teach our children well.

We hope that you'll find *Making Scripture Memory Fun* a useful and fun resource as you seek to write God's Word on the hearts of children.

VISUAL-SPATIAL

Resistible Rainbows

> *"I have set my rainbow in the clouds, and it will be the sign of the covenant between me and the earth."*
>
> GENESIS 9:13

SUPPLIES: You'll need a Bible, newsprint, a marker, white paper, crayons, dark watercolor paint, paintbrushes, and water.

Have the children sit in a circle. Print the memory verse on the newsprint. Read the verse aloud with the children. Say: **This verse comes at the end of the story of Noah. Let's see if we can remember what happened in the story. I'll start by asking the question, "What happened first?" Then the person on my right will tell what he or she thinks happened first. Then I'll ask the next person, "Can you think of anything in the story that happened before that?" and "What happened next?" This way we'll be sure not to leave anything out of the story.**

Have the children tell the story of Noah and the ark. At the end, ask:

● **Is there anything else we should remember about the story of Noah?**

● **The verse we're learning today says that the rainbow was a sign of a covenant or promise. What was that covenant—what did God promise to do?**

● **What do you know about the promises God makes?**

Say: **God never breaks his promise. Let's make reminders of this verse to help us remember that God always keeps his promises.**

Distribute paper and crayons, and have the children draw rainbows. Make sure they create brilliant rainbows by pressing hard with the crayons. While the children are coloring, frequently get their attention and have the class recite the verse with you. Children may also want to print the verse on their papers with crayon.

When the rainbows are finished, pass out paintbrushes, dark watercolor paint, and water. Have the children paint their entire papers with the paint. Ask:

● **What happened to the rainbow when you painted over it with the dark paint?**

Say: **Even though this paint is dark, it can't cover up the rainbow. No matter what, God's promises always remain true. God will always keep all** of his promises. **Every time we see a rainbow, we can remember that it's a sign of God's covenant. Rainbows can also remind us that God keeps his promises. Let's say the verse together again.** Say the verse again with the children.

Naturalistic

He's a Rock

> *"The Lord lives! Praise be to my Rock! Exalted be God, the Rock, my Savior!"*
> **2 SAMUEL 22:47**

SUPPLIES: You'll need a Bible, markers, small sheets of poster board, and access to an area with lots of rocks. You might also need a small shovel or trowel.

Take children to an outdoor area where rocks and dirt are found. Bring your Bible with you. Invite each child to find one rock and one dirt clod, and then ask the children to stand in a circle. If children are having difficulty finding dirt clods, simply dig a small hole in the ground, and have the children make their own dirt clods. Ask:

● **Which will hold you up if you stand on it—a rock or a dirt clod? Explain why.**

● **What will happen if you try to stand on the dirt clod? Why?**

Say: **A solid rock holds together and is strong enough to hold us up if we stand on it. The dirt clod just crumbles. The Bible talks about God being our rock. Let's listen to 2 Samuel 22:47.**

Have a volunteer read the verse; then ask:

● **How is God like a rock?**

● **Why does that make God a Savior?**

● **What can we do to thank God?**

Have children form four groups. Give each group one sheet of poster board and a marker. Have one child in each group write a section of the verse on the poster board. Divide the verse in this way:

Group 1: The Lord lives!

Group 2: Praise be to my Rock!

Group 3: Exalted be God, the Rock,

Group 4: My Savior!

Have everyone stand in a circle. Ask children to place their rocks on the ground in front of them. Have each group read its phrase out loud (with feeling). Let the other groups echo the phrase after each group reads. Whenever the word "rock" is mentioned, ask the children to gently step up onto their rocks and then back into place.

After reading the entire verse once, ask the members of Group 1 to pick up their rocks and share one reason they want to thank God for being their rock and Savior.

Continue through at least four rounds until each group has had an opportunity to share.

BODILY-KINESTHETIC

Two-Ton Pencils

> "But as for you, be strong and do not give up, for your work will be rewarded."
> 2 CHRONICLES 15:7

SUPPLIES: You'll need a Bible, a pencil, and a snack for each child.

Have the children form a circle, standing at least an arm's length from their neighbors. Give each child a pencil (unsharpened if you are with very young children). Explain that the pencils each weigh two tons—which is approximately the same amount as twenty-five grown-ups weigh.

Demonstrate how heavy a two-ton pencil would be by immediately letting yours fall to the floor and then pretending you can barely lift even one end of the pencil. Huff, puff, and grimace. Really get into the role: Your enthusiasm makes this activity fun for your children—and guarantees they'll participate, too.

Ask children to take turns "lifting" their pencils in a way that makes pencils look like they weigh two tons. Say: **As each person lifts a pencil, I want the rest of us to say 2 Chronicles 15:7 together, "But as for you, be strong and do not give up!" Let's practice once. Good! Ready?**

One at a time, encourage kids to make a dramatic show of lifting their pencils. Have children repeat the phrase as each child takes a turn, and have children affirm all efforts with applause.

When the last child has performed, say: **Now repeat after me: "But as for you, be strong and do not give up** (pause and let children repeat) **for** your work will be rewarded" (pause). **Now here's your reward: a snack!**

Gather children for a snack, and as you do so, ask them to repeat the entire verse with you several times.

While children are enjoying the snack, say: **We had a lot of fun pretending the pencils were so heavy that we couldn't lift them. But there are things we do in real life that we really struggle with. Sometimes we have to learn new skills that are hard. Sometimes we have to take a stand for what is right when everyone else is doing wrong. Sometimes we have to humble ourselves, say we're sorry, and ask for forgiveness. All of these things are hard, and sometimes we might want to just give up.** Ask:

● **Have you ever had to do something that was so hard you wanted to give up? Tell us about it.**

● **In what ways does God give us strength?**

● **In what ways does God reward us when we work hard?**

Say: **One of the gifts God gives us is other Christians who can support and encourage us when things are tough. When we feel like giving up, our Christian friends can give us the help and encouragement to keep us doing what God wants even when we want to give up. Let's encourage each other with this verse.**

One by one, put your hand on each child's shoulder and have the entire class say the verse to him or her. For example, you would put your hand on Barry's shoulder. Then everyone would say, "But as for you, Barry, be strong and do not give up, for your work will be rewarded."

❖ Reflective

Wants and Needs

> *"The Lord is my shepherd, I shall not be in want."*
>
> **PSALM 23:1**

SUPPLIES: You'll need Bibles, pencils, and paper. You may also need toy catalogs and glue.

Give each child a pencil and a piece of paper. Say: **Let's write wish lists of things we'd like to receive for birthday presents or Christmas.**

Pretend that there's no limit on the cost of the presents—you can ask for anything.

You may want to have several toy catalogs available to help with ideas. If you are working with young children, let them tear out pictures of toys they would like and glue these to their papers. After a few minutes, have the children read their lists to the rest of the group. Then ask:

- **How did you decide what to put on your list?**
- **What was similar or different about our lists?**
- **After hearing everyone else's lists, how would you change what you'd want to receive as a present?**

Give the children a second sheet of paper, and say: **Now let's make a different kind of list. Let's pretend that each one of you is stranded on your own desert island. You're going to be there for the rest of your life—there's no possibility of being rescued. If you could take ten things with you, what would you take? Remember, your survival may depend on the things you take.**

After several minutes, have the children read their lists to the rest of the group. Ask:

- **How did you decide what to put on your list?**
- **What was similar or different about our lists?**
- **After hearing everyone else's lists, how would you change what you'd want to take with you?**

Have the children set their lists aside. Open your Bible to Psalm 23:1, and read it aloud. Have the children repeat the verse. Then ask:

- **What does the word "want" mean in this verse?**
- **What is the difference between a want and a need?**

Have the children open their Bibles to Psalm 23. Read the entire psalm aloud. Then give the children time to read and ponder the entire psalm on their own. Give the children each a third sheet of paper. Say: **Let's make a third list. Write down the things that God promises to provide for us. Think about these questions as you create your list:**

- **How can God provide for our needs?**
- **Why does God provide for our needs?**
- **Why are there people who are still in need?**

Give the children a few minutes to write and think. Then ask the children to share their discoveries about God's provision. Then have each child share his or her list with the class. After each child shares, have the class recite the verse together.

House Designers

> "Surely goodness and love will follow me all the days of my life, and I will dwell in the house of the Lord forever."
>
> **PSALM 23:6**

SUPPLIES: Each child will need a sheet of white paper, a pencil. You'll also need a Bible, a chalkboard and chalk or newsprint and a marker, rulers, and crayons or colored pencils.

On the chalkboard or newsprint, draw a large rectangle, and print the word "house" inside. Next put a roof on the house by drawing a triangle on top of the rectangle. Following the lines of the drawing, print the verse along the roof and sides of the house.

Allow the children to examine the drawing; then have the entire class read the verse aloud as you point out the words. Then say: **If you "dwell" someplace, it means that you live there. So this verse says, "I will live in the house of the Lord forever.** Ask:

● **What do we usually call the people who live in a house together?**

Say: **People who love God and who are Christians are part of God's family. They can say this verse. Let's say it together.** Say the verse aloud with the children. Ask:

● **What do you think it means when it says "surely goodness and love will follow me all the days of my life"?**

Say: **Let's think a little about the house of the Lord. I'll give you paper, pencils, and crayons or colored pencils, and I'd like each of you to pretend you're an architect. Your job is to design God's house. You can either draw what you think the house looks like from the outside, or you can draw a floor plan of the house that shows the size, shape, and use of each room inside. While you're creating, think about how you can illustrate the first part of the verse: "Surely goodness and love will follow me all the days of my life."**

Give each child a sheet of paper and a pencil. Also provide rulers and markers. Allow children ten or fifteen minutes to work on their drawings. Older children will enjoy going into great detail and may want even more time. Every two or three minutes catch the children's attention; then point to the "verse house," and have everyone repeat the verse. Encourage children to copy the verse on their papers.

To conclude, let the children take turns showing and describing their houses. After each child shares, repeat the verse together.

Naturalistic

In the Bag

> *"The earth is the Lord's, and everything in it, the world and all who live in it."*
>
> PSALM 24:1

SUPPLIES: You'll need a Bible, paper lunch sacks, and access to a park or wooded area.

Visit a park or wooded area—or even the church lawn—with your group, and don't forget to bring your Bible. Provide one paper lunch sack for each child. Say: **We're going to see how much we can stuff in our sacks today. The only rule is everything you put in your sack needs to be something that belongs to God. You might pick up some grass or dirt or whatever else you see that you think belongs to God. You'll have ten minutes.**

Walk with the children as they begin their collections. Caution the children about approaching potentially dangerous natural objects such as poison ivy, beehives, wasp nests, fire anthills, or any wild animal. Encourage the children to include as many different objects as they can find. When the time is up, call the group together and sit in a circle.

Invite each child to share one item from their sacks with the rest of the group. Then ask:

● **Why do these things belong to God?**

Open your Bible to Psalm 24:1, and have one of the children read it out loud. Ask:

● **According to this verse, what belongs to God?**

Say: **Wow! Everything belongs to God. The whole world belongs to him. Let's keep sharing what we've found, and we'll remind each other who it all belongs to.**

Give children a chance to share items from their sacks one at a time. After each child shares an item, ask:

● **Who does this belong to?**

Repeat the verse together after each child shares. Then ask:

● **Why do you think God made this?**

Continue until children have shared the contents of their sacks.

🖐 BODILY-KINESTHETIC

Over the River and Through the Woods

> *"Show me your ways, O Lord, teach me your paths."*
>
> PSALM 25:4

SUPPLIES: You'll need a Bible.

Have the children form a line, as if to play Follow the Leader. You'll take the Leader spot.

Say: **Let's use our imaginations and act out a story. Pretend that God took us on a hike this afternoon. We followed God like you're following me.** (March around the room.) **At first we walked through pleasant meadows.** (Stop and encourage the children to tell you what they see in the meadow.) **We were so busy looking at the beautiful meadow that we forgot to follow God, our leader. When we looked up, we didn't know which way to go, so we called out, "Show me your ways, O Lord, teach me your paths."** (Have the children call out the verse.) **And God found us and led us to the path.** (Start walking again.)

Then we crossed over a cold stream, hopping from rock to rock. (Hop from spot to spot.) **We hiked up a little hill.** (Lean forward as you walk.) **Then we crossed over a river by balancing our way across a fallen log.** (Step heel-to-toe with your arms outstretched.) **Then we picked our way up a mountain trail. Way up on our right** (point and look up), **there was nothing but a towering cliff. Way down on our left** (point and look down), **there was a sudden drop off. It was scary and we were afraid. "Was this really the right path?" we wondered. So we called out again, "Show me your ways, O Lord, teach me your paths."** (Have the children call out the verse.) **And God reassured us all we needed to do was follow him.** (Start walking again.)

Up and up we climbed on the narrow path. Sometimes other paths branched off from our trail. (Stop walking.) **They looked easier, and we**

wanted to walk down them. But we knew God was our leader so we called out, "Show me your ways, O Lord, teach me your paths." (Have the children call out the verse.) And God encouraged us to keep following him up and up on the narrow, steep path. (Begin walking again.)

Finally we came to a beautiful mountain meadow. The sun was shining, and it was warm. We were tired. So we lay down to take a little nap. (Lie down.)

Soon, we were asleep. (Snore.)

When we woke up. it was completely dark. We'd slept all afternoon. The night was cold and moonless. The temperature had dropped, and we were shivering. (Shiver.)

And listen (cup hand to ear): There were wolves howling, and they were getting closer!

We had to get out of here, but how? We couldn't tell which way to go. We didn't know how to find the path. And we couldn't find our leader. So we shouted, "Show me your ways, O Lord, teach me your paths." (Have the children call out the verse three times.)

And then we looked beside us, and there was God, our leader. He'd been right there with us all the time. And God led us down the path and safely home.

Gather children around you and discuss:

● When this verse talks about the path, it doesn't really mean a hiking trail. What do you think it means when we ask God to show us his ways and to teach us his path?

● Why is it wise to shout to God when we don't know what to do?

Say: We can be confident that when we call out to God, he answers our call. He'll show us the way to follow him!

Close in prayer, thanking God for his faithfulness.

✦? REFLECTIVE

Wait for the Lord

> "Wait for the Lord; be strong and take heart
> and wait for the Lord."
>
> **PSALM 27:14**

SUPPLIES: You'll need a Bible for each child, a chalkboard and chalk or newsprint and a marker, a watch with a second hand, and red construction paper.

Give each child a Bible, and then ask:

● **When you do have to wait?**

● **What are some things that are hard to wait for?**

Then say: **Sometimes waiting is hard. Let's see how good you are at waiting. On "go" I'll start keeping time on this watch. When you think one minute is up, shout out, "Wait for the Lord!" Let's see how good you are at waiting until the time is up.**

Wait until one minute is up. Then call time. Ask:

● **Was a minute shorter or longer than you expected? Explain.**

Have the kids find Psalm 27:14 in their Bibles. Read the verse together aloud. Say: **Now, I'll keep time again for one minute. While you are waiting for it to go off, think of as many things as you can that you have to wait for.**

When the time is up, write on the chalkboard or newsprint a list of everything the kids could think of that they have to wait for. Read Psalm 27:14 together again aloud. Ask:

● **Why do you think God wants us to wait?**

● **What kinds of things do you think God wants us to wait for?**

● **The verse says to wait for God. What should we wait for God to do?**

Then say: **I'll keep time again for one minute. This time, think of as many things as you can that are strong. For example, a person who can lift one hundred pounds is strong! Or, a magnet can be strong.** Wait until one minute is up. Call time and write the list of strong things next to the first list on the chalkboard. Read Psalm 27:14 again together aloud. Ask:

● **Why does this verse talk about being strong? What does that have to do with waiting?**

● **There's another expression in this verse. The verse says "Take heart and wait for the Lord." What does "take heart" mean?**

Give each child a piece of red construction paper. Then say: **Let's wait for one minute one more time. This time, tear your piece of construction paper to create a heart before the time is up.**

When one minute is up, call time. Have the children recite Psalm 27:14 from memory. Point to the paper heart and the lists on the chalkboard, using them as visual cues to help the children remember the verse.

Close with the following prayer: **God, it is difficult to wait for you. Help us to be strong and take heart and wait for you in our lives. Amen.**

⅞ Logical-Mathematical

Forever Plans

> *"But the plans of the Lord stand firm forever, the purposes of his heart through all generations."*
>
> **PSALM 33:11**

SUPPLIES: You'll need a Bible, a chalkboard and chalk or newsprint and a marker, pencil, and paper.

Say: **I've got a challenge for you. I'd like for you to think of at least one thing on the earth that has existed for two thousand years without any change.**

Write the children's ideas on the chalkboard or newsprint. Then go back and consider each idea to determine if it really has remained unchanged for the last two thousand years. For example, while the mountains have stood for two thousand years, the trees are not the same and the path of the streams has changed the shape and size of the canyons. After you've considered each item on the list, ask:

● **What has this activity taught you about the nature of our world?**

Say: **There's a verse in the Bible that talks about something that lasts forever. Let's read Psalm 33:11.** Read Psalm 33:11, and write it on the chalkboard. Have the children read the verse aloud. Ask:

● **What kinds of plans does God make?**

● **What does "the purposes of his heart" mean?**

● **When you see that "the plans of God stand firm forever," what does that tell you about God's nature or personality?**

- Why can God make plans that will last forever?
- How do God's plans differ from your plans?

Say: **Let's think about specific plans God has made or purposes of his heart that will last forever.**

Have the children brainstorm. Plans might include God's plan for bringing people close to him or God's plan for his Word to last forever. Purposes might include God's intention to be loving and forgiving. As each child mentions one of God's plans or purposes, have the entire class recite the verse together. Continue until everyone has shared.

♫ MUSICAL

Jars of Tears

> *"The Lord is close to the brokenhearted and saves those who are crushed in spirit."*
> **PSALM 34:18**

SUPPLIES: You'll need a Bible, newsprint, a marker, eight glass jars, a container of water, and metal spoons.

Have kids discuss the following questions with a partner:
- **What kinds of things make you feel sad?**
- **How can you tell if someone is feeling sad?**
- **Tell about a time you felt sad. What did you do?**

After kids have discussed the questions, call them back together, and invite them to share their responses. Record their responses to the first question on a sheet of newsprint.

Say: **Sometimes when we're sad, we feel like we're all alone. It seems like no one understands how sad we are. But the Bible says God understands, and he's with us when we're sad. Listen to what Psalm 34:18 says about God and our sadness.**

Read the verse; then have children repeat it once with you. Say: **Some things make us just a little bit sad. For example, if you dropped your ice-cream cone on the ground, you might frown or pout. But other things make us so sad that we feel like crying all day long. Let's rank the sad things on our list from least sad to most sad.**

Help children rank the items on their list. Invite a child to draw a single sad face next to the least sad item. Have another child draw two sad faces next to the second least sad item. Continue until you've ranked the eight saddest items on the list.

Tear the items apart, and put the top eight sad items on a table with one sad item next to each glass jar. Set a container of water nearby. Have kids find their partners and stand next to one of the jars. If you have more than sixteen students, you'll need to form trios or foursomes for this part of the activity.

Say: **When we're sad, the Lord is close to us whether we cry a little or a lot—or even if we don't cry at all. Let's say the verse together as a reminder.** Recite the verse with the children. **Fill your jar with the amount of water "tears" you think you'd cry in that situation. Then we'll turn our jars of tears into water chimes and set our verse to music.**

Help children fill their jars so that each jar has a different amount of water. Hand out spoons. Then show the children how to take turns playing their "chimes" by gently tapping the jars with the spoons.

Say: **In all our sad situations, God is close to us. Let's sing about that now.**

Help children compose a tune using all the chimes. (If you include one note for the Scripture reference, you'll be able to play each chime twice.) Then sing the song several times.

NaTuRaListic

To the Skies

> *"Your love, O Lord, reaches to the heavens, your faithfulness to the skies."*
>
> **PSALM 36:5**

SUPPLIES: You'll need a Bible; white kitchen trash bags; scissors; and sun, moon, star, and heart stickers. You'll also need access to a large gym or playing field.

Before this activity cut a small opening at the closed end of each trash bag large enough for a child's head to fit through. Then make armholes in the sides. You'll need trash bags for half of the group.

Ask children to help you create "heavenly" costumes. Place the prepared trash bags on the floor, and ask the kids to decorate them with the sun, moon, and

star stickers. Don't place the heart stickers out with the rest. You'll need them for later in the game.

Ask a child to read Psalm 36:5 out loud. Repeat the verse once for the children; then ask:

- **How high does the Lord's love reach?**
- **How high is that?**
- **How high can God's faithfulness go?**
- **How high up is the sky?**

Say: **We're not sure how high the sky is, are we? It seems like it goes up and up forever. And that's just like God's love. It goes on and on forever.**

Invite the children to play a game that is "way out." Explain that this game will allow the children to share God's love and try to reach the skies at the same time. You'll need to play this game in a large open area such as a gym or playing field. Designate a starting line and designate a finish line about thirty yards away. Older children can play on a larger field.

Have the children form two groups—the Heavens and the Loves. Let the Heavens put on the heavenly costumes. Give each member of the Loves a heart sticker. On "go" have the Heavens run toward the finish line, while the Loves chase them. When a Love catches a Heaven, have the Love put his or her heart sticker on the Heaven. Then have both kids continue to race toward the finish line.

When all the kids have reached the finish line, have everyone call out the verse. Then have all the untagged Heavens raise their hands. If there are untagged Heavens, begin the game again, and have everyone run toward the starting line, even the tagged Heavens and the Loves who don't have stickers any-more. When they all arrive at the starting line, call out the verse again. If there are still untagged Heavens, have kids run the other direction again. Continue until all the Heavens have been tagged with a heart sticker and everyone has found out that God's love truly does reach the heavens!

 **LiNGUiSTiC**

Hope-Finders

> *"But now, Lord, what do I look for? My hope is in you."*
>
> PSALM 39:7

SUPPLIES: You'll need a Bible, chalkboard and chalk or newsprint and a marker, pencils, and paper.

Write out the words to Psalm 39:7 on the chalkboard or newsprint; then ask:
● **What is a riddle?**

● **Who can share a riddle or joke they know with the rest of us?**

Encourage the kids to tell several knock-knock jokes or other riddles they may know. Say: **Psalm 39:7 is kind of a riddle, but it's not a funny riddle. This kind of riddle tells us something important about God. Let's study it. The person who wrote the psalm, the psalmist, asks "What do I look for?"** Ask:

● **What are some things we look for?**

● **What do you think the psalmist was talking about?**

Say: **The psalmist goes on to answer his own question by saying "My hope is in you."** Then ask:

● **How does the sentence, "My hope is in you," answer the psalmist's question?**

● **Sometimes people put their hope and trust in things other than God. What kinds of things do people put their hope and trust in?**

Say: **In the verse that comes right before this one, the psalmist talks about some of the things people put their hope and trust in. He says that people work and hurry, but their efforts go for nothing; that people heap up wealth, and then they die, and the money goes to someone else. Then comes verse 7, the verse we're learning today. In this verse the psalmist is really saying that it's silly to look for happiness or hope in anything other than God. He's saying, "Why would I look to anything but God? Nothing is as good as God. My hope is in God."**

Say: **We're going to write some hope-finders using the same style this psalmist used. First we're going to write a couple of sentences about where people look for happiness. Then we'll write out Psalm 39:7 to show where true hope and joy can be found. For example, you might write, "Some guys work out every day trying to be the best basketball** player. They think if they can be like Michael Jordan, they'll have it made. 'But now, Lord, what do I look for? My hope is in you.' " Hand out paper and pencils, and give the children several minutes to write their hope-finders. Encourage each child to write more than one. Then have each child read his or her hope-finders aloud.

Then pray: **God, thank you for being trustworthy. We know it's better to put our hope and trust in you than in anything else in this world. Help us to remember every day to put our hope in you. Amen.**

MUSICAL

A Mighty Fortress

"God is our refuge and strength, an ever-present help in trouble."

PSALM 46:1

SUPPLIES: You'll need a Bible, a chalkboard and chalk or newsprint, and markers.

Before class, copy the words to the first verse of the hymn "A Mighty Fortress Is Our God" on a chalkboard or newsprint. (See the chart on page 27.)

Have a volunteer read Psalm 46:1; then have kids repeat the Bible verse together. Kids may not be familiar with the word "refuge." Explain that a refuge is a safe place, such as a basement during a tornado. Remind children that God is a refuge for us in the midst of trials. Ask:

● **When have you been in trouble?**
● **Did God help you? Explain.**

As kids share about their times of trouble, encourage them to look for ways God may have helped them—even if they didn't realize it at the time. After a few minutes of discussion, say: **Hundreds of years ago, a man named Martin Luther wrote a song about the way God helps us. Martin Luther was a great Christian leader, and God helped him through a lot of very hard times.**

Teach kids the tune and words to "A Mighty Fortress Is Our God." Sing the song a few times. Be sure to explain the meaning of any words kids may not understand. (Refer to the chart on page 27.) Tell the children the other three verses of the song explain that in the battle between God and Satan, Satan will lose.

Show the children that you can replace the words "A mighty fortress is our God, a bulwark never failing" with the words of the verse: "God is our refuge and our strength, an ever-present help in trouble."

Have the kids form pairs. Hand out newsprint and markers to each pair. Have pairs write their own words to complete the song, using the Bible verse as the first line of their new versions of Martin Luther's song.

When everyone is finished, have the class sing each pair's song.

Then close with a prayer similar to this one: **God, we thank you for being our refuge and our strength. Please be present with us whenever we experience trouble this week. In Jesus' name, amen.**

"A MIGHTY FORTRESS IS OUR GOD"
in Contemporary Language

A mighty fortress is our God, **A bulwark never failing;**	God is like a mighty castle, a strong, defensive wall that will never fail.
Our helper He, amid the flood **Of mortal ills prevailing.**	God will help us through the many trials of life that seem to flood over us.
For still our ancient foe **Doth seek to work us woe;**	For Satan, our enemy from ancient times, is still working to make us miserable.
His craft and power are great,	Satan has many abilities and he is strong.
And, armed with cruel hate, **On earth is not his equal.**	One of his weapons is hate. We need to take him seriously.

Clean Hearts

"Create in me a pure heart, O God, and renew a steadfast spirit within me."

PSALM 51:10

SUPPLIES: You'll need a Bible, glass windows, and dry-erase markers.

TEACHER TIP

There are many musical versions of this Scripture passage. If you have a tape or CD of any of these songs, bring it in and play it for the children. For many students, combining the visual learning experience with the musical learning experience will greatly enhance their understanding of this verse. It will also help them remember the verse.

Look up and read Psalm 51:10 with the children. If the children don't know the word "steadfast," look it up in the dictionary, or explain that the word means loyal or faithful.

Say: **In this psalm, the psalmist is asking God to forgive him for the sins he has committed.**

Ask:

● **What is a pure heart?**

● **Why do you think the psalmist wanted a pure heart?**

● **What is a steadfast spirit?**

● **Why do you think the psalmist wanted a steadfast spirit?**

Say: **Think about what a pure heart and a steadfast spirit would look like. We're going to draw pictures of a pure heart and a steadfast spirit on the windows with markers. The light will shine through our drawings and make them look like beautiful stained-glass windows.**

Hand out dry-erase markers, and have the children draw pictures of a pure heart and a steadfast spirit on the windows. To illustrate a steadfast spirit, children might draw an image that is "steady" and "unmoving" such as a rock or a mountain. The children could also draw someone they know who has a steadfast spirit.

Also have the children write out the verse and decorate the words. As the children work, periodically get their attention, and have them recite the verse together.

When the drawings are finished, have the children sit where they can gaze at the pictures. Have them explain what they've drawn. Then ask:

● **When a person has a pure heart and a steadfast spirit, how do they act? think? talk?**

28

● How can a person develop a pure heart and a steadfast spirit?

Say: **Let's pray this verse to God as a way of asking him to develop in us a pure heart and a steadfast spirit.**

Pray the verse together three times.

 **REFLECTIVE**

God's Mighty Deeds

> *"I will meditate on all your works and consider all your mighty deeds."*
>
> **PSALM 77:12**

SUPPLIES: You'll need a Bible, a chalkboard and chalk or newsprint and a marker, paper, and colored pencils or markers. You'll also need a tape player and some meditative music.

Write out the words of Psalm 77:12 on a chalkboard or newsprint. Have the children read aloud the verse together. Explain that the word "meditate" means to think on or to consider. Ask:

● **Why is it important to meditate on God's mighty deeds?**

Hand out paper, and provide colored pencils or markers. You'll need enough colored pencils so that each child can use several colors.

Say: **Write the words of Psalm 77:12 on the top half of your paper. Use colors that will make the words meaningful to you. For example, you might write the word "works" in green because green reminds you of the world, which is one of God's works.**

Give the children a few minutes to accomplish this. Then say: **Let's take some time to meditate on and consider God's mighty deeds just as this verse tells us to. Divide the rest of your paper into two sections. In one section write out all of the works and mighty deeds you can think of. Then take some time to meditate and consider all the things you've written down—think about what these things tell you about God. In the second section, write down your conclusions. Write down what you've learned about God from meditating on his works and mighty deeds.**

Play meditative music while the children work. Periodically stop the music, and have the children recite the verse together.

After several minutes, stop the activity and have volunteers tell you what they've discovered about God. Then close by reciting the verse together.

♫ MUSICAL

Joyful Songs

> *"Worship the Lord with gladness; come before him with joyful songs."*
>
> **PSALM 100:2**

SUPPLIES: You'll need a Bible, a CD or cassette of praise songs, and a CD or cassette player.

Form pairs. Say: **Sing a few lines of your favorite praise song for your partner. Then tell your partner why you like that song, and what it means to you.**

Allow a few minutes for kids to describe their songs; then call everyone back together. Ask:

● **What do we sing about when we sing praise songs?**

● **How do you feel when you sing a praise song by yourself? With other people?**

● **Why is singing a good way to praise God?**

Say: **In Psalm 100:2, the Bible tells us: "Worship the Lord with gladness; come before him with joyful songs." Let's say that together.** Lead children in repeating the verse; then continue: **God has given us so many good things. Singing joyful songs about God's goodness is a great way to thank God for all the good things he's given us. Let's choose some joyful songs we can sing together now.**

Play the cassette or CD you've brought and let kids vote on which songs they think are the most joyful. Sing the joyful songs together as a class, or offer to lead another class in worship using the songs you've chosen. Recite the memory verse together in between each song. Then close your worship time by repeating the verse together.

 **MUSICAL**

Sing Your Thanks

> *"Enter his gates with thanksgiving and his courts with praise; give thanks to him and praise his name."*
>
> PSALM 100:4

SUPPLIES: You'll need a Bible, newsprint, and a marker.

Have kids sit in a circle so that everyone can see the newsprint. Read Psalm 100:4; then have kids repeat it once with you.

Say: **When the Bible talks about entering God's gates, it's talking about entering the temple gates to worship God. Today we come to church to worship God. So since we've already "entered his gates," let's express our thanksgiving to God for all the good things he's done for us.**

We'll go around the circle and each share one thing we're thankful for. Instead of saying the things we're thankful for, we'll sing them. You can use part of a familiar tune, or make up your own. After you sing what you're thankful for, I'll write it on the newsprint, and we'll all sing it back to you.

Demonstrate by singing "Thanks for my family" to the tune of the first line of "Three Blind Mice." Encourage children to help each other come up with new tunes each time. For familiar tunes, remind them they can use praise songs, nursery rhyme tunes, or even advertising jingles.

After everyone has sung their thanks, read the verse again. Then have kids try to sing through the whole list. Have each item's creator be prepared to prompt the group if necessary.

 **MUSICAL**

Sounds of Anger, Sounds of Love

> *"The Lord is compassionate and gracious,*
> *slow to anger, abounding in love."*
>
> PSALM 103:8

SUPPLIES: You'll need a Bible; a dictionary; and various sound-making items found in your room, such as chairs, pencils, paper, or a stapler.

Have kids form pairs to discuss the following questions:

● **What makes you angry?**

● **When you get angry, what do you do?**

● **When you get angry, do you feel really mad all of a sudden, or does your anger build up inside for a while? Explain.**

Invite kids to share their responses; then say: **It's a good thing God doesn't get angry like we do. Listen to what the Bible says about God's anger.**

Read Psalm 103:8. Say: **The Bible says God is slow to get angry. It also says God is full of love. We've already talked about our anger. Now let's talk with our partners for a few minutes about loving feelings**. Have pairs discuss the following questions:

● **When you're full of love, what loving actions do you do?**

● **How do you feel while you're showing love to someone?**

● **How do you feel when someone shows love to you?**

Invite kids to share their responses; then say: **There are two other words in this verse that describe God. The verse says God is compassionate and God is gracious. Talk with your partner about what it means to be compassionate. Then talk about being gracious.** Ask:

● **In what ways is God gracious?**

Provide a dictionary for children to look up the words "compassionate" and "gracious" if they want to. Give the children a few minutes, and then invite them to share their responses. Say: **Now work with your partner to create sounds to express all four of these feelings: compassion, grace, anger, and love. You can use any materials you can find in the room, including yourself and your partner.**

Help children create their compassionate, gracious, angry, and loving sounds. For example, for angry sounds, suggest harsh or sudden noises such as pounding a chair on the floor or scraping fingernails on a chalkboard. For loving, compassionate and gracious sounds, suggest softer noises such as sighing, tapping two erasers together or stroking a person's hand.

After pairs have created their sounds, call everyone back together. Have children say the verse together. Each time you repeat the verse, have a different pair demonstrate their sounds as you say "compassionate," "gracious," "anger," and "love."

 LinGuistic

The Storytelling Surprise Ball

> *"Sing to him, sing praise to him; tell of all his wonderful acts."*
>
> **PSALM 105:2**

SUPPLIES: You'll need a Bible, thick yarn (preferably in blue or green) and small items that represent God's creation. Collect items such as pebbles; shells; leaves; flowers; nuts; tiny pine cones; and miniature toy or craft items such as animals, people, and bugs. Try to have at least one item per child.

Beginning with one of the items, wrap the yarn around several times until you can't see the item any longer. Add another item and wrap the yarn again until that item disappears. Continue to do this until all the items have been hidden into the ball of yarn.

Gather the children together. Hold up the ball of yarn, and say: **This is a Storytelling Surprise Ball. We're going to pretend that the ball is the earth. We'll use it to tell stories about the wonderful world that God created.**

Read Psalm 105:2 from the Bible. Say: **This verse praises God and says to tell others of the wonderful acts of God. One of those acts was the creation of the world.**

Teacher Tip

You can also choose items for the Surprise Ball that show other kinds of wonderful acts such as God's miracles or God's personality.

Explain that the children will take turns unwinding the ball until an object appears. When an object is found, the child who unwound the yarn will tell a quick story about the object. They may tell stories from their own experiences or make up stories.

For example, if a child finds a pebble, he or she might say, "One day I found a beautiful pebble at the lake. I couldn't believe how smooth it was. I mailed it to my Grandma since she likes to put pebbles on a shelf in her kitchen." If the child finds a sheep, he or she might say: "Once upon a time this sheep gave some wool, and the wool was made into blankets to keep lots of people warm."

As soon as the child has told the story the rest of the class will chant the verse with the rhythm shown below.

Sing to him, sing praise to him; tell of his wonderful acts.

Make comments and ask questions to prompt children who may be having trouble coming up with stories. When the Surprise Ball is completely unwound, say: **You may keep the object you found in the Storytelling Surprise Ball. Show it to your family and friends as you tell them about God's wonderful act of creation.**

If you have time and enough supplies, you can have the children make their own Surprise Ball to take home. Each child can personalize it with items that show God's wonderful acts.

LinGuistic

The Praise-Phrase Orchestra

> *"Praise the Lord. Give thanks to the Lord, for he is good; his love endures forever."*
>
> **PSALM 106:1**

SUPPLIES: You'll need a Bible and a short stick or dowel to be a conductor's baton.

Begin by asking a child to read the verse from Psalm 106:1. Say: **This verse can be divided into three phrases. I'll say them, and you repeat them after me. "Praise the Lord."** (Pause.) **"Give thanks to the Lord, for he is good."** (Pause.) **"His love endures forever."** (Pause.) Ask:

● **Why is it important to praise God?**

● **How do our praises benefit God? benefit us?**

Have the children form three groups. Assign one of the phrases to each group. Ask each group a question about its phrase:

Group 1: **What are some ways you can praise God every day?**

Group 2: **How is God good to you?**

Group 3: **What are some ways God's love lasts forever?**

Say: **Now I'm going to turn you into the Praise-Phrase Orchestra. I'll be the conductor, and when I point to your group, I want you to say your phrase. Begin by whispering your phrase and saying it a little louder each time.**

Point the baton, with great gusto, at the groups when it's their turn. Continue until the children are saying their phrases in loud voices.

Then say: **That was great! Let's try something else.**

Assign each group a different phrase from the verse. Then say: **This time begin by saying your phrase really slow. Each time we go around, say it a little faster.**

You can also add in crescendos (getting gradually louder), decrescendos (getting gradually softer), sforzandoes (sudden accents), staccato phrases (short choppy sounds), and legato phrases (sweet and smooth sounds) if you feel comfortable with these.

After you have conducted, let some of the children take a turn at being the conductor.

If time permits, let each group set its phrase to a tune and conduct the orchestra this way.

When finished, say: **Usually, the audience applauds the orchestra. But today, let's applaud our audience—God.**

Have the children applaud.

 **INTERPERSONAL**

Generosity Jeopardy

> *"Good will come to him who is generous and lends freely, who conducts his affairs with justice."*
>
> **PSALM 112:5**

SUPPLIES: You'll need a Bible, a sheet of newsprint, a marker, pencils, and paper.

Write the verse on a sheet of newsprint, and post it on the wall. Say: **A famous preacher a long time ago gave his people some rules about money. He said there were three of them: earn all you can, save all you can and give all you can. What do you think of this advice to Christians?** Allow children to give their responses.

Say: **Psalm 112:5 says, "Good will come to him who is generous and lends freely, who conducts his affairs with justice." If I were to ask you to answer the question "Why is it a good idea for Christians to earn all they can, save all they can, and give all they can?" with an answer that comes from the Bible, you might tell me about Psalm 112:5. You might say, "Because, 'Good will come to him who is generous and lends freely, who conducts his affairs with justice.'" That promise from the Bible might help me want to be a generous person.** Ask the kids the same question, and have them repeat the Bible verse to you, with the reference.

Say: **That same Bible verse might be a good answer for other questions, too. I'd like for each of you to choose a partner. You and your partner will come up with some other questions that could be answered by this Bible verse. Come up with several questions because we'll be using the questions to play a game.**

Have children form pairs. If you have a mixed age group, assign young partners to create a foursome with older partners. Give each pair or foursome a piece of paper and a pencil. The person wearing the most blue will be the recorder (who writes the questions), and the person wearing the least blue will be the reporter (who will ask the question to the rest of the class). If the kids are having trouble coming up with questions, you might prompt them with the following ideas:

- **"Why should I loan my bike to my sister?"**
- **"Why is it a good idea to give a pencil to a kid in my class who lost his?"**
- **"Why should I put part of my allowance in the offering?"**

After the pairs have all thought of several questions, bring the class back together and form two groups. Make sure that pairs stay together and that they bring their lists of questions. Explain that in the game "Jeopardy!" someone gives an answer to a question, and the other person has to tell the question. Then play a game of Generosity Jeopardy. Have one group play the role of Alex Trebek. That entire group will call out the verse in unison. Let members of the other group respond with one of its questions. Then have the groups switch roles. Continue until the groups both run out of questions.

Reflective

No Fear

> *"The Lord is with me; I will not be afraid.*
> *What can man do to me?"*
>
> **PSALM 118:6.**

SUPPLIES: You'll need a Bible, chalkboard and chalk or newsprint and a marker.

Have the kids sit on the floor. Ask:
- **What are you afraid of?**
- **How do you feel inside when you are afraid?**
- **What makes your fear go away?**

Open the Bible and write Psalm 118:6 on the chalkboard or newsprint. Then say: **The Bible has good news for us about fear. Let's read this verse together.** Have the children recite Psalm 118:6. **Everybody gets scared, but this verse promises that no matter what, God is always with us. We don't have to be afraid.**

The last sentence of this verse is puzzling. Let's see if we can figure out what it means. We all know that sometimes bad things happen and sometimes we get hurt. But the last sentence of this verse seems to say that other people can't really harm us. Ask:

● **What do you think the last part of the verse means?**

Say: **Maybe what this verse is saying is even if things go wrong, God is still there. Maybe it means nothing is so terrible that it will destroy us. God is ultimately in charge, and God is stronger than the bad things that might happen. In the end, God will make things turn out all right.**

Let's think about some situations when we might be afraid. I'll read the situation aloud while you close your eyes and pretend it's happening to you. After each one, we'll say the verse together as a reassurance that God's in control.

Have the children lay down and close their eyes. Read the following situations aloud.

Say: **Pretend it is very dark outside. The neighborhood street light at the end of the block is burned out. You stayed out playing with your friends a little too long. Now you know you have to walk two blocks home in time for dinner. You know that your mom is probably really worried about you. She's probably even mad because you stayed out so late. You've never been out this late before. The neighborhood looks so differ- ent at night. You come up to the corner where you know you need to cross the street. Just then, an unfamiliar car stops and the door opens. A man you don't know asks if you are lost. "Do you need a ride?" he offers. Now a little voice inside of you remembers that you should never ride with strangers. But then the man says, "It's OK, I'll take you home. You can trust me." You say...**

Encourage the kids to open their eyes and say Psalm 118:6 at this time. Discuss the situation with the kids as to what they should do if they were in this situation. Then have them close their eyes again, and continue with the following situation, encouraging the kids to again say Psalm 118:6 aloud whenever they are afraid.

Say: **You're sitting in school one afternoon doing your math. Your mind begins to wander over the morning's events. You had gotten up, made your bed, gone into the kitchen and decided to make your own toast for breakfast. Oh no, you can't remember unplugging the toaster. You're mom always said to remember to unplug it because the cord has some loose wires. Oh well, it will probably be OK until you get home. Then you can unplug it before your mom comes home from work and sees that you forgot.**

The school bell rings, and you dash out of school, in a hurry to get home. As you run down the street, you hear sirens. "There must have been an accident at the corner down the street," you think. As you round

the corner to your house, you see the fire trucks going in the same direction. Now you can smell smoke. And then you see your house. Flames are shooting out of the kitchen windows. The firefighters are pulling out the hoses and beginning to fight the fire. Just then your mom drives up in the car to meet you when you get home from school; you say...

Encourage the kids to say Psalm 118:6. Then discuss the situation talking about what they should do in this case.

Have the children relate stories about times when they've been afraid. At the end of each story, have the entire class repeat the verse together.

End with a prayer about fear and learning to count on God when we are afraid.

 **LinGuiStic**

Diamond Poems

> *"I rejoiced with those who said to me, 'Let us go to the house of the Lord.'"*
>
> **PSALM 122:1**

SUPPLIES: You'll need a Bible, a chalkboard and chalk or newsprint, paper, pencils, and markers.

Begin by asking a child to read Psalm 122:1 from the Bible. Write the verse on a chalkboard or newsprint; then ask children to read it along with you. Say: **This verse is from the book of Psalms. Many people like to think of the psalms as beautiful poetry that expresses many different feelings to God.** Ask:

● **What feeling does this verse express?**

● **We call the person who wrote the psalm the psalmist. Why do you think the psalmist rejoiced when he came to God's house?**

● **What do you like about coming to church—or our house of the Lord?**

● **What makes this church different than other churches?**

Tell the children to close their eyes as you ask them to think about their church:

● **What are the sounds you hear there?**

● **How does it smell?**

- **What colors and designs do you see?**
- **Do you ever taste anything at church? Explain.**
- **How do the walls and doors and pews feel?**

Say: **Thousands of years ago, the writer of Psalm 122 wrote about going to the house of the Lord. Today, we're going to write poems about our church.**

Pass out papers, pencils, and markers. Tell the children that their poem, when finished, will form the shape of a diamond. Say: **Just as a diamond is valuable to its owner, our church is valuable to all of us who worship here. We're going to write "diamond poems" in honor of our church.**

Guide them in writing the poem in this form:

LINE ONE: Write the word "church."

LINE TWO: Write two words that describe the church.

LINE THREE: Write three words about what happens at church.

LINE FOUR: Write two words telling how you feel when you are in church.

LINE FIVE: Write the word "church."

Here is an example of a diamond poem about a church:

Church
Old, Stone
Worship, Singing, Prayer
Joyful, Special
Church

With younger children, write the poems as a class.

When the children are finished, point out how their words form a diamond shape. Some may want to copy their poems over or draw a line around the poem to create a more pronounced diamond. Ask them to write the verse at the top or bottom of their papers. If time permits, they may decorate the area outside of the diamonds with drawings of the church or with more words that describe their feelings about the church.

Have the children read their poems to the rest of the class. After each child reads his or her poem, have the rest of the class recite Psalm 122:1 together.

Consider hanging the poems on a bulletin board or wall for all to see. The diamond poems, when put into a booklet, also make a nice gift for your group to present to your pastor or to honor a member of the church on a special occasion. Some of the children could make a cover for the booklet with the verse printed on it.

VISUAL-SPATIAL

Filled With Joy

> *"The Lord has done great things for us, and we are filled with joy."*
>
> **PSALM 126:3**

SUPPLIES: You'll need a Bible, blank overhead transparencies, paper towel tubes or toilet paper tubes, tape, permanent markers, tissue paper, and small candies. Cut the transparencies in half widthwise. Cut the paper towel tubes in fourths or the toilet paper tubes in half. Each child will need one transparency half and two cardboard tube sections.

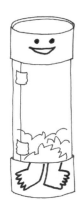

Give each child a transparency half and two cardboard tube sections. Have the children roll up their transparencies and slide them through the cardboard tubes as though they were placing a napkin ring on a napkin. Have them position the tubes at either end of the transparencies. Have the children tape the tubes in place and then put another strip of tape along the seam of the transparencies.

Then hand out markers, and have the children draw their own faces on the top cardboard tubes and their legs and feet on the bottom cardboard tubes.

Give each child a small piece of tissue paper to crumple up and stuff in the bottom end of the tube.

Have each child bring his or her creation and sit in a circle on the floor with you. Say: **Each of you has made a tube person that's decorated to look like you. But all of the people you made are empty—you can see right through them! We're going to fill them up with something. I'll read a Bible verse that will tell you what we're going to fill them up with. Listen closely and see if you can figure out what we'll fill our people with.** Read aloud Psalm 126:3 and have the children repeat it. Ask:

● **According to this Bible verse, what should we fill these people with?**

Bring out the bowl of candy, and say: **We're going to let this candy represent our joy. We'll show that we're full of joy by filling our people full of candy.** Ask:

● **The Bible verse says God has done great things for us—what kinds of great things has God done for you?**

For each thing the children mention, have them each put one piece of candy in their tube people. With each piece of candy, have the children recite the verse. Continue until the tube people are full of candy.

End with a prayer of thanksgiving for God's good gifts and the joy that we are all filled with.

INTERPERSONAL

Unity Tag

> *"How good and pleasant it is when brothers live together in unity."*
>
> **PSALM 133:1**

SUPPLIES: You'll need spools of thread, a whistle or other attention-getting device, and access to a large open area.

Say: Psalm 133:1 says, "How good and pleasant it is when brothers live together in unity!" Unity means that we have the same purpose or that we work together toward the same goal. Today we're going to play a game that requires a lot of unity!

Have the kids get into groups of three. Choose one group to be the Taggers. Have the Taggers link arms to form a circle. Tie a double piece of thread at waist level around the other groups. Tie the thread tightly enough so the thread won't fall from the children's waists, but not so tightly that it will be binding.

Tell the children that the goal of the game is to avoid being tagged and to avoid breaking the thread. Give the groups one minute to determine a strategy for how to avoid the Taggers. Tell the children that whenever you blow the whistle, they must freeze in place and recite the verse.

Then start the game. Tell the children that they'll have more success if they move slowly and smoothly. Whenever a group breaks its thread or gets tagged, blow the whistle. Have all the children freeze and recite the verse. The group that was tagged or broke its thread will become the new Taggers. Tie thread around the previous group of Taggers, and have the new Taggers link arms. While this is going on, give the other players a minute to readjust their strategies for moving in unity. Restart the game. Play until all the groups have been Taggers.

Then call all the groups together. Ask:

● **How did your group decide to move in unity?**

- What kind of things did you have to consider?
- When did you find it easiest to move together? hardest?
- What were some benefits of moving together?
- How is this like trying to work together in unity in real life?
- What are the difficulties we face when we try to live in unity with each other?
- Why do you think the Bible uses the words "good" and "pleasant" to describe living in unity?

Have the children get back in their trios. Have each group member say the verse aloud and tell the others one way they can live in unity at school or home.

Naturalistic

Wonderful Kids

> *"I praise you because I am fearfully and wonderfully made; your works are wonderful, I know that full well."*
>
> **PSALM 139:14**

SUPPLIES: You'll need a Bible and access to an open room or gym.

Have children form a circle in a gym, open room, or outside on a sunny day. Ask the kids to think for a moment about all the wonderful things they can do. Suggest ideas such as walking, running, jumping, or hopping. Then read aloud Psalm 139:14.

Say: **God's works are wonderful. People are one of God's works. God has made us able to do amazing things! We can jump up high.** (Have children jump up.) **We can hop on one foot.** (Have children all hop.) **We are fearfully and wonderfully made! Let's find out what you can do.**

Let children take turns naming things that they can do, such as somersault, run, or twirl. As each child names an action, let him or her lead the group in doing the action while saying the verse out loud. Let the leader lead the group once around the room or gym; then let the next child tell an action and act as leader. Continue to help the children repeat the verse until each child has led the group. Ask:

- How does the verse describe God's works?
- What was your favorite thing that we did? Explain.

● Why is it important to thank God for making us so special?

Say: **Let's remember to thank God every day for how wonderfully he made us. Saying this verse while you pray is a wonderful way to say thank you to God.**

Naturalistic

Heavenly Praise

> *"Praise him, sun and moon, praise him, all you shining stars."*
>
> PSALM 148:3

SUPPLIES: You'll need a Bible, tape, newsprint, markers, and a large room.

Print the verse on newsprint, and tape it on the wall. Have the children read the verse aloud together. Ask:

● **What kinds of things are in outer space?**

● **What is mentioned in our Bible verse?**

● **How can the sun, moon, or stars praise God?**

Say: **Let's find out how they praise God by setting up our own solar system. We'll need someone to be the sun. Another person can pretend to be the earth, and another one will be the moon. The rest of us will be stars.**

Help children take their places with the sun in the center of the room, earth walking around the sun, while the moon walks around earth. Let the other children stand in different places while they "twinkle" by holding their hands above their heads and moving their fingers. Once the solar system is in place and working, have everyone repeat the verse. Let children continue to rotate while you ask:

● **How do the sun, moon, and stars praise God?**

● **What did he create them to do?**

Say: **God made the sun to shine and give warmth to the earth. He made the earth to revolve around the sun, and our moon to rotate around the earth. He made all the stars to shine. By being what they were meant to be and doing what God intended, they praise him.**

Have children repeat the verse twice more while they continue to rotate. Then invite children to sit in a circle. Ask:

- What did God create us to do?
- How can we praise him?
- What will you do today to "shine" and give God praise?

Let children write their names around the verse on newsprint. Then allow them to decorate the newsprint with drawings of the sun, moon, and stars.

VISUAL-SPATIAL

A Lamp and a Light

> *"For these commands are a lamp, this teaching is a light, and the corrections of discipline are the way to life."*
>
> **PROVERBS 6:23**

SUPPLIES: You'll need a Bible, a chalkboard and chalk or dry-erase board and marker, tape, and several strings of Christmas lights.

Write the verse on the chalkboard or dry-erase board. Then tape one string of Christmas lights around the chalkboard.

Gather the children near the chalkboard. Turn off the room lights and turn on the Christmas lights. Give the children a moment to read the verse. Then say: **This verse comes from the book of Proverbs. Proverbs are wise sayings that teach us the right way or the best way to live. When this verse talks about "these commands," it is referring to the rules and commands our parents give us. This verse uses a metaphor, a word picture, to help us understand the importance of rules. It calls commands a "lamp" and teaching a "light."**

- **In what ways are your parents' commands and teaching like a lamp or a light?**

Say: **One way to explain this verse is to say that rules are like a light because they show us the way to live wisely in the same way that a street light or a car's headlights show us where the road goes.**

Close your eyes and imagine you're in this situation: You're riding in a car late at night out in the country. It's a very dark night. It's cloudy and you can't see the moon or the stars. You're on a winding road and you aren't familiar with it. The headlights of the car are dim, and it's hard to make out the road. You become worried because there are sharp drop-offs

on both sides of the road. If the driver can't see the road, he might drive off the road and go over the side of the cliff. You sit on the edge of your seat and peer at the road. You want to do everything you can to help the driver stay on the road. Ask:

- **How does this story relate to rules and commands being like a light?**
- **What were the dangers in the story?**
- **What are the dangers of not following rules?**

Say: **Let's say the verse together.** Recite the verse with the children. The next part of this verse says, "The corrections of discipline are the way to life." Ask:

- **What do you think this means?**

Say: **Our parents give us rules and teachings to help us know what is right and wrong. When they correct us or discipline us, they're helping us become people who live right, who are responsible and who are self-controlled. Living right is like being on the right path. The rules light up the path.**

Have the children create a path on the floor around the room with the rest of the Christmas lights. For each light bulb in the Christmas lights, have them mention one rule, command, or teaching they get from their parents that illuminates the right way to live. One by one, have the children walk along the path they've created. As each child finishes the path, have the entire class repeat the memory verse.

LinGUiSTiC

Search It Out

> "He who seeks good finds goodwill, but evil comes to him who searches for it."
>
> **PROVERBS 11:27**

SUPPLIES: You'll need a Bible, newsprint, a marker, pencils, paper, and photocopies of the "Search It Out" word search from page 48. Cut the word lists off of the bottom of the handouts, and cut apart the lists of evil words from the lists of good words.

Hand each child a copy of the "Search It Out" word search. Give half of the children the "good" word list. Give the other half of the children the "evil" word list. Don't tell the children they have different lists. Give the children three to five minutes to find all the words on their lists. Explain to them that words can appear across, down, diagonal, or backward. (The solution can be found on pg. 64.)

Then say: **I gave out two lists of words—a list of "good" words and a list of "evil" words. Let's make a list of all the words that you found. First let's list all the words that the kids with the "good" words found.**

List all of the words they found on a sheet of newsprint. If they mention some of the evil words, write those in a separate column.

Say: **Now let's list all of the words that the kids with evil words found.**

List these words on a sheet of newsprint. If they mention some of the good words, write those in a separate column. Ask:

● **What did you think when you saw words in the puzzle that weren't on your list?**

Say: **I find it interesting that those of you who were supposed to find good words found more good words than evil words. And those of you who were supposed to find evil words found more evil words than good words. In fact, many of you passed over or ignored any words you found that weren't on your list.** Ask:

● **Why do you think you passed over words you found that weren't on your list?**

Say: **There's a Bible verse that talks about finding what we search for. Let's read Proverbs 11:27.** Look up the verse and have one of the children read it aloud.

Say: **Let's all read that verse together. Those of you who had the good word list will say the first part of the verse. Those of you who had the evil word list will say the second part of the verse together.** Have the children say the verse several times. Then ask:

● **How does your experience with the puzzle relate to this Bible verse?**

● **Why do you think that people who seek good will find good and people who seek evil will find evil?**

Say: **Let's write action plans. Action plans tell us what we're going to do. The plans that we're going to write will explain what we're going to do as a result of learning this verse. First write the verse at the top of your paper. Then write, "Therefore, I will…" Complete the sentence with at least three different specific things you can do to search for good instead of evil.**

Hand out paper and pencils, and have the children write action plans that list at least three specific things they can do to search for good and avoid evil. For example, a child might write "Therefore, I will spend time every day reading my Bible, I will listen to my parents more and I won't watch television shows that are too violent."

Have the children read their action plans to at least four other people. Each time they read their plans, have them also read the verse.

Search It Out

H	D	P	E	A	C	E	B	D	O	P	H	S	I	W	R	P	S	Y	S	I	L
L	J	M	G	E	W	N	C	B	E	F	L	O	U	C	A	R	E	N	T	O	A
E	O	K	B	G	T	E	O	R	I	D	A	E	X	U	M	I	C	O	E	P	I
D	C	V	T	U	S	W	I	O	G	T	J	G	H	Z	E	L	P	M	A	V	U
X	B	H	E	O	V	A	L	K	L	I	V	S	O	D	H	R	O	K	L	E	Q
N	R	J	I	K	H	M	A	E	V	H	T	I	D	N	U	O	W	B	Y	L	G
Q	G	O	S	S	I	P	T	N	I	R	O	X	U	F	V	E	J	A	T	U	I
V	W	I	J	U	Q	A	K	P	Y	P	A	T	I	E	N	C	E	P	H	L	U
F	O	A	S	E	G	I	T	R	V	E	W	U	K	H	A	O	M	O	L	N	E
J	T	B	V	R	W	R	E	O	S	D	O	D	H	F	E	F	Y	L	S	I	W
L	Y	P	U	X	O	K	I	M	E	R	I	N	U	L	I	E	R	N	E	P	T
P	R	D	K	E	A	P	R	I	Z	F	G	S	A	S	X	O	B	E	R	G	H
T	G	M	F	Y	N	T	I	S	E	S	A	B	C	I	T	H	G	I	V	O	N
E	M	L	E	P	O	H	W	E	V	O	I	G	E	O	D	U	B	D	I	F	E
I	Q	N	A	C	N	Z	O	F	T	O	R	B	A	N	U	L	T	O	C	K	C
W	V	F	O	R	G	I	V	E	N	E	S	S	D	I	B	R	U	J	E	O	N
H	E	J	B	E	A	V	Y	D	S	H	U	P	T	E	C	J	A	H	Z	Q	E
U	Y	S	J	N	T	U	N	D	E	R	S	T	A	N	D	I	N	G	R	U	L
R	X	U	E	Y	I	W	U	R	K	L	U	P	L	E	U	F	L	K	E	R	O
T	J	I	A	R	S	G	Y	E	I	D	I	S	H	O	N	O	R	E	W	O	I
D	O	R	S	I	P	A	N	O	L	U	R	F	E	S	I	B	T	C	A	F	V
L	P	Z	I	W	O	H	M	E	J	I	D	G	L	I	T	A	E	H	C	R	O

UNDERSTANDING	LOVE	STEAL	GOSSIP
CARE	HELP	LIE	HIT
PATIENCE	HOPE	HURT	GRUDGE
HUG	PRAY	CHEAT	DISCOURAGE
JOY	SERVICE	BROKEN PROMISE	WOUND
FORGIVENESS	PEACE	VIOLENCE	DISHONOR

BODILY-KINESTHETIC

Deep and Wide

> *"The prudent see danger and take refuge,*
> *but the simple keep going and suffer for it."*
> **PROVERBS 27:12**

SUPPLIES: You'll need a newspaper, masking tape, and a simple snack such as cookies.

Spread several sheets of newspaper on the floor to cover an area at least 4x7 feet. Use masking tape to attach the newspaper sheets to each other and to the floor.

Gather everyone on one side of the newspaper and form two groups: the Prudents and the Simples.

Explain to the children that the word "prudent" means wise, and that the word "simple" means not understanding much. Ask the Prudents to stand on your left, and the Simples to stand on your right.

Tell this story and have your children act it out.

Say: **The Prudents and the Simples went on a picnic one day. The Prudents walked up a path and saw a deep ravine. They came to the edge and looked down. Then they looked at each other and said, "The prudent see danger and take refuge!"**

Ask the Prudents to walk to the opposite edge of the newspaper, peer over the edge, and repeat the phrase several times. Then have them back away from the edge of the newspaper and sit down.

Say: **Then the Simples came along on their way to the picnic. They saw the deep ravine. They came to the edge and looked down. Then they looked at each other and said, "But the simple keep going and suffer for it."**

Have the Simples walk to the edge of the "ravine," peer over the edge, and pretend to step off the cliff and fall into the ravine. Have the Simples repeat their phrase several times from their places at the "bottom" of the ravine.

Have the groups trade places and repeat the activity. Then have everyone sit on the newspaper to enjoy a picnic snack.

Before serving the snack, have everyone repeat the entire verse three times together with you.

During your snack ask:

● **What did the Prudents do to show they thought ahead to avoid danger?**

● **What did the Simples do to show they didn't understand what would happen?**

● **What is something dangerous in your life? How can you be prudent about it?**

Naturalistic

Withering Weeds

> *"The grass withers and the flowers fall, but the word of our God stands forever."*
>
> ISAIAH 40:8

SUPPLIES: You'll need a Bible, index cards, pens, and glue sticks. Plan to do this activity the day after the church's grass has been mowed, or simply choose a tall grassy area that needs mowing.

Walk with the children through a grassy meadow or lawn. Remember to bring your Bible with you. Encourage the children to sit in the grass and invite them to pick up dry or broken pieces of grass or flowers. If there are dandelions or clover nearby, warn the children to check for bees before picking any blossoms.

Open your Bible to Isaiah 40:8, and ask a volunteer to read the verse. Ask:

● **What happens to grass when it is picked like we've just done?**

● **What will happen to the flowers in your hands?**

Say: **Grass dries up and flowers die, don't they? They don't last very long.** Ask:

● **What would happen if it got very cold? How would that change the grass?**

● **What if it didn't rain for a long time? What would the grass look like?**

Have the volunteer read the verse aloud again. Ask:

● **What is one thing that will last forever?**

Say: **Grass dries up and blows away in the wind, but we can count on the Bible to be true forever.**

Ask the group to sit in a circle on the grass. Instruct each child to pick up a handful of grass and a flower (if possible). Place the Bible in your lap and pick up a handful of grass and a flower. Say the verse with the group while you do these actions:

"The grass withers (let the blades of grass fall to the ground)
and the flowers fall (drop the flower),
but the Word of our God (pick up the Bible)
stands forever"
(Isaiah 40:8).

Place the Bible in the lap of the child to your right and have the group repeat the words as he or she does the motions. Continue until everyone has done the motions.

Give each child an index card and a pen. Have them write the verse on their cards. Provide glue sticks, and encourage children to glue a few blades of grass and a flower onto their cards as reminders that those things won't last, but God's Word stands forever.

VISUAL-SPATIAL

Clay Pots

> *"Yet, O Lord, you are our Father. We are the clay, you are the potter; we are all the work of your hand."*
>
> ISAIAH 64:8

SUPPLIES: You'll need a Bible, self-hardening clay, and a chalk-board and chalk or newsprint and a marker.

Give each child a chunk of clay about the size of a golf ball. Say: **You have five minutes to turn your hunk of clay into some useful object such as a cup, a bowl, or an artistic sculpture.**

While the children are working, write the memory verse on a chalkboard or a sheet of newsprint. When the children are finished, have them each show the class what they've made. Ask:

● **What did you think about while you were creating your clay sculpture?**
● **How did you decide what to make?**
● **What are your plans for your sculpture? What will you do with it?**
● **Are you pleased with what you've created? Explain.**

Say: **The verse I've written on the chalkboard is about making things out of clay. Let's read the verse together.** Have the class read Isaiah 64:8. Ask:

● **What does this verse mean when it says that we are the clay and God is the potter?**

● **What do you think God's plans were when he made us?**

● **Why do you think God chose to make you just as you are?**

● **What do you suppose God thinks about his creation?**

Say: **Let's say the verse again.** Recite the verse with the children. Say: **This verse says that each one of us is a work of art. Because God is great and wonderful, his creations are beautiful. Just as your clay creation is a result of your own intelligence, creativity, and personality, we, as God's creation, show God's intelligence, creativity, and personality.**

This verse also says that we have purpose. When a potter creates a pot or a mug, he or she has a purpose in mind for it. God has a purpose in mind for each of us. Let's thank God for creating us and ask him to show us what purpose he has in mind for us.

Go around the room and have the children all recite the verse as a prayer for each child. For example, for Christine, the class will pray, "Yet, O Lord, you are Christine's Father. Christine is the clay, you are the potter, Christine is the work of your hand." When you've prayed the verse for each child, pray: **God we thank you for creating us. Help us to know what your purpose for us is. Thank you for making us the work of your hand. Amen.**

ReFLective

Making Plans

> *"'For I know the plans I have for you,' declares the Lord, 'plans to prosper you and not to harm you, plans to give you a hope and a future.'"*
>
> JEREMIAH 29:11

SUPPLIES: You'll need a Bible, copies of a blank calendar page for the upcoming month, pencils, paper, a chalkboard and chalk or newsprint, and markers.

Give each child a copy of the blank calendar page for the upcoming month and a pencil. Then say: **Write down all of the plans that you already know** about for the month to come. **Be sure to include all of your soccer practices or music lessons on the right day so that you won't miss any. Don't forget holidays and birthdays. Write down each and every plan you already have for the month to come.**

Allow a few minutes for children to think and write.

Then give each child a sheet of blank paper, and say: **Now, let's think about more long-term plans. Write down these questions and spend the next few minutes answering them:**

● **What would you like your life to be like in high school?**

● **What would you like your life to be like ten years after high school?**

Have the children jot down words that show the plans they'd like to make for their future, such as driving a car, going to college, or becoming an astronaut. While the kids are writing down their plans, write Jeremiah 29:11 on the chalkboard or newsprint.

Have the children describe to the rest of the class what they'd like their lives to be like in the future. Then ask:

● **What were you thinking as you wrote down your plans for the month and as you considered your future?**

Say: **It's fun to think about all the great things that might happen to us in the future. But sometimes it's a little scary to think about the future. There are lots of things to think about, and it can be hard to make decisions. And while we like to think about all the good things that will happen, there will also be sad things. But God's Word gives us hope. Jeremiah 29:11 tells us what God thinks about us and our future. Let's read it together.**

Have the children read the verse aloud.

● **How does this verse affect how you feel about your future?**

Have the children each think of one word that represents a plan they have for themselves or that expresses their excitement or apprehension about the future.

Let each child write his or her word on the chalkboard around the verse. After each child writes his or her word, have the rest of the class affirm that person by stating the child's name and then reciting the verse together. For example, Chris may write the word "car" to represent plans to drive. Have the class say, "Chris, 'for I know the plans I have for you,' declares the Lord, 'plans to prosper you and not to harm you, plans to give you a hope and a future.' "

What's His Name?

> *"He who forms the mountains, creates the wind, and reveals his thoughts to man, he who turns dawn to darkness, and treads the high places of the earth—the Lord God Almighty is his name."*
>
> **Amos 4:13**

SUPPLIES: You'll need a Bible, newsprint, masking tape, index cards, and markers.

Tape five large sheets of newsprint around the room. Label each sheet of newsprint with a number (1 through 5) on an index card taped above it. Have the murals progress sequentially around your room. Place markers on the floor beneath each mural.

Have children form five groups. Ask each group to stand near a different mural.

Open your Bible to Amos 4:13, and ask one of the children to read the passage aloud.

Say: **We're going to illustrate this verse. It paints pictures with words to describe some of God's creations. Each group will illustrate one phrase from the verse. While you are drawing, think of who made all of this wonder.**

Assign the phrases as follows:

Group 1—He who forms the mountains

Group 2—Creates the winds

Group 3—And reveals his thoughts to man

Group 4—He who turns dawn into darkness

Group 5—And treads the high places of the earth

Ask one child from each group to write the group's phrase in big letters at the top of the newsprint. Explain to Group 5 that the word "tread" means to walk.

Explain to the kids that while they are working on the pictures, you will ask, "What's his name?" several times. That's their cue to say the verse together. To help the kids learn the verse, have them read from the murals.

Once the pictures are complete, have children walk single file around the newsprint murals. As the class passes each mural, have everyone say the phrase out loud. Continue until all five phrases have been repeated; then ask, "What's his name?" and have the children say the final phrase of the verse.

⊚ VISUAL-SPATIAL

Light Show

> *"Let your light shine before men, that they may see your good deeds and praise your Father in heaven."*
>
> MATTHEW 5:16

SUPPLIES: You'll need a Bible, a chalkboard and chalk or newsprint and a marker, at least one flashlight with a strong beam, and a box. You'll also need an inexpensive flashlight or a liquid crystal glow-stick for each child.

Before the activity, print the memory verse on a chalkboard or newsprint. Put the flashlights or glow-sticks in a box next to the chalkboard.

Gather the children and darken the room as much as possible. Ask:

● **What is it like to be in the dark?**

● **Which of our senses is most affected by darkness?**

Say: **In the dark, it's hard to see what we're doing and it's hard to see what anyone else is doing. The Bible says that when people do wrong, they like to do it in the dark where no one else can see it.** Ask:

● **Why do you think people do wrong things in the dark?**

Say: **People like to hide the wrong things they do because they're ashamed of them. Think about wrong things that you've done.**

● **Have you ever wanted to hide them? Explain.**

● **What have you done to hide your wrong actions?**

Say: **Now think about the good things that you do. When we do good things, we want other people to see them and take notice of them. We're proud of the good things we do, so we do them in the light where everyone can see.** Ask:

● **How do you feel when others notice your good deeds?**

Say: **We're going to learn a Bible verse that talks about doing good deeds. It's Matthew 5:16. Let's read it together.** Shine your flashlight on the board, and have the class read the verse together.

Say: **Let's celebrate our good deeds. Think of something good that you've done, and raise your hand when you've thought of one. When I call on you, tell us what you've done. I'll write your idea on the board while you come and get a flashlight out of the box. Turn your flashlight on and shine your light around the room. Be sure you don't shine the light in anyone's eyes.**

Have each child mention a good action and choose a flashlight out of the box. When everyone has a flashlight, say: **Now I want everyone to sit or lie down on the floor because we're going to make a light show. Follow my directions:**

Shine your light in the center of the ceiling.

Now point your light at the verse. Let's say it together. (Say the verse.)

Shine your light in all the corners of the room twice.

Now point your light at the verse. Let's say it together. (Say the verse.)

Draw a star with your light.

Now point your light at the verse. Let's say it together. (Say the verse.)

Pretend to paint a wall with your light.

Now point your light at the verse. Let's say it together. (Say the verse.)

Point your light on the floor and make the light move like ocean waves.

Now point your light at the verse. Let's say it together. (Say the verse.)

Now shine your lights every which way.

Now point your light at the verse. Let's say it together one last time. (Say the verse.)

BODILY-KINESTHETIC

Rest Stop

> *"Come to me, all you who are weary and burdened, and I will give you rest."*
> MATTHEW 11:28

SUPPLIES: You'll need paper, markers, and tape. Make these four signs and hang each one in a corner of your room to create four activity centers: Friendship Center, Grade Center, Muscles Center, and Rest Stop.

Rush through the first part of this activity as quickly as possible. You want children to feel that they can't quite keep up with you.

Stand in the Rest Stop activity center, and have children gather in the Friendship Center to your immediate right. Tell the children that today they'll work hard to make friends, get good grades, and develop their muscles. They'll start by making friends.

In the Friendship Center, ask kids to shake as many people's hands as they can in thirty seconds. Tell them there are only two rules: They can't shake the same person's hand twice in a row; and when they shake hands, they must say, "Pleased to meet you." When thirty seconds are up, have the children hurry to the Grade Center.

At the Grade Center, they'll answer questions you ask from your corner. Ask the following questions quickly, without giving children enough time to answer. You may need to adjust the questions to be age-appropriate for the children you have in class:

- **How much is two plus two?** (4)
- **What is the capital of Michigan?** (Lansing)
- **George Washington was born in what year?** (1732)
- **In 1861, who was the king of Italy?** (Victor Emmanuel II)
- **How many squares are on a checkerboard?** (64)
- **What is 327 times 47.5?** (15,532.5)
- **What is the square mileage of the country of Ecuador?** (109,483)

Then urge children to quickly dash to the Muscles Center where they'll quickly follow your instructions. Make sure the kids keep up the physical activity until their hearts are beating quickly.

- **Touch your noses!**
- **Touch your toes!**
- **Touch your elbows!**
- **Jump up and down five times!**
- **Turn in a circle five times to your left!**
- **Turn in a circle five times to your right!**
- **Skip over here!**

When children reach the Rest Stop, let them collapse on the floor and rest. Then, gently and quietly say: **"Come to me, all you who are weary and burdened, and I will give you rest."** You may need to say it several times to establish a mood of quietness after the rush of the activities. Keep your voice quiet and gentle so that the children experience quiet and rest as their heartbeats slow to normal.

Collapse on the floor with your children, and say: **Jesus said this. The people he said it to were also tired. They were tired of trying to please God by working hard to always do and say the right things. No matter how hard they tried they couldn't get everything right!** Ask:

- **How is that similar to or different from this activity?**
- **In your real life, what do you work hard at?**

After each response, have everyone recite the verse together. Then say: **Think about all the ways you get weary or tired during the week.**

Pause for a moment, then have the children recite the verse together. Then say: **Think about all the ways you are burdened—that means it feels like you're carrying a heavy load—because you're sad or angry.**

Pause for a moment, then have the children recite the verse together. Ask:
- **Why do you think Jesus offers us rest?**
- **What does God's rest feel like?**

Say: **Our God is good and gracious—God is always ready to give us what we need. This verse tells us to stop working hard to provide ourselves with the things we need. This verse tells us to come to Jesus and Jesus will take away our tiredness, our weariness, and our burdens, and he will turn around and give us wonderful rest. What a good promise. Let's say the verse together one more time.**

Have the children recite the verse with you.

BODILY-KINESTHETIC

Gathering Game

> *"For where two or three come together in my name, there I am with them."*
>
> **MATTHEW 18:20**

SUPPLIES: A handkerchief, poster board, a marker, and access to a large room or safe outdoor area.

Do this activity in a large room or a safe outdoor area.
Print the verse on the poster board, and invite the children to read it aloud with you.

Say: **Jesus said that when we come together as Christians, he is with us. That's one reason why Christians believe it is important to spend time with other Christians. To help us remember this, we're going to play a game.**

Have the group stand in a circle. Choose one person to walk around the outside of the circle with the handkerchief. Tell the child to drop the hanky behind someone. As soon as the hanky is dropped, have everyone except the chosen child run to the far reaches of the room or play area. After everyone has dispersed, call the group back by saying, **Come together.**

As the children re-form the circle, hold up the poster board, and lead the group in reading the verse.

To continue the game, ask the child who now holds the hanky to take a turn walking behind the circle to drop the hanky. Then have all children disperse until you call them together. Repeat the cycle until all children have had a turn. Be sure to end each round by saying the verse.

Finally, invite the group to sit down, and then ask:

● **How did you feel when you stayed in the middle of the room and everybody else was far away from you?**

● **How did you feel when we came together again?**

Say: **Now that we've all come together again, let's bow our heads and talk to Jesus who is here with us.**

Pray: **Dear Jesus, thank you for promising to be with us when we gather together. Help us to recognize your presence every time we're together. Amen.**

Reflective

Heart, Soul, and Mind

> *"Love the Lord your God with all your heart and with all your soul and with all your mind."*
>
> MATTHEW 22:37

SUPPLIES: You'll need a Bible, a chalkboard and chalk or newsprint and a marker, paper, and colored pencils or markers.

Hand out paper and pencils or markers. Ask:

● **What is your definition of the word "love"?**

Have the children write their definitions on the papers. Then have the children share their answers. Ask:

● **Why is love necessary?**

Write out the words of Matthew 22:37 on a chalkboard or newsprint. Have the children read aloud the verse together. Then encourage the kids to use the following actions as they repeat this verse a second time.

"Love the Lord your God	(point upward)
with all your heart	(touch your heart with index finger)

with all your soul   (touch the center of your chest)

and with all your mind."   (Touch your forehead.)

Ask:

- **What does this verse mean?**
- **Why is it good to love God?**

Hand out a new sheet of paper to each child. Then say: **Imagine what the world would be like if everyone loved God with all of their heart, all of their soul, and with all of their mind.** Use the hand actions as you repeat the verse. **On your piece of paper, create a picture or a description of what the world would be like if everyone loved God above everything else.**

Give the children a few minutes to create their pictures or write their descriptions. Then encourage them to share their drawings with the rest of the class by explaining what is special about their love-filled worlds. Encourage the children each to name one small act of love they could do to help the world become more like the one in their pictures. For example, they might be able to pick up trash each day as they walk home from school, as a love-filled world might not be dirty.

After each child shares, have the class repeat the verse with the actions. Then pray, asking God to help you show with your actions how much you love him.

✳ LOGICAL-MATHEMATICAL

Who's Great?

> *"The greatest among you will be your servant. For whoever exalts himself will be humbled, and whoever humbles himself will be exalted."*
>
> **MATTHEW 23:11-12**

SUPPLIES: You'll need a Bible, index cards, and pencils.

Give each child ten index cards and a pencil. Say: **Today we're going to talk about what makes a person popular or important. Think about the important and popular kids at your school. Then write down ten characteristics that make people important or popular at school. Write one characteristic on each card. After you've written your characteristics, put the**

cards in order from most important to least important.

Give the children a few minutes to write and prioritize the cards. Then have the children get with a partner and compare their lists. After a few minutes, ask:

● **In what ways were your lists similar? different?**

● **In general, how would you describe a popular or important person in your school?**

Say: **Let's read what the Bible has to say about being important.** Read Matthew 23:11-12. Then have the children slowly recite it with you. Pause after each sentence or phrase, and emphasize the words "greatest," "exalts," "humbled," "humbles," and "exalted." Ask:

● **What do you think this verse means?**

● **How would you define the word exalt?**

● **What do you think it means to humble oneself?**

Say: **Let's make new lists. Think about what would make a person important and popular with God. Turn your cards over, and write down ten characteristics and then put them in order from most important to least important.**

Distribute more index cards and give the children a few minutes to write down characteristics on the cards and prioritize them. Get their attention several times during the activity, and have the entire group recite the verse. After the children have worked for a few minutes, have them get with the same partner as before and compare their lists. After a few minutes, ask:

● **How would you describe a person who's important in God's eyes?**

● **How is this person similar to or different from the person who's important at school?**

● **Why do you think God's idea of an important person is so different from the world's idea of an important person?**

● **What can you do to be the kind of person God is pleased with?**

End this activity by saying the verse together one more time. Then pray and ask God to help you be the kind of people who please God.

LinGuiStic

Good News!

> *"Go into all the world and preach the good news to all creation."*
>
> **MARK 16:15**

SUPPLIES: You'll need a Bible; a globe or a world map; and a snack with a Danish (cookies or pastries), Brazilian (pineapple and banana slices), or French (cheese and bread) "flavor."

In this activity, children will learn to say "good news" in three different languages: Danish, Portuguese, and French. If there is someone in your congregation who speaks another language, consider asking him or her to translate "good news" for you in that language, or to come and teach the words to the children. Consult with your guest about an appropriate snack.

Gather the children together. Hold up the globe and say: **Here is the world that God made! Look at all the water, and look at all the countries. We're going to play the Spin-and-Name game. You'll each get a chance to close your eyes, spin the globe, and point to a country. Then say or read the name of that country.** If children touch water, they are to spin again until they touch a country.

If you're using a world map instead of a globe, have the children close their eyes and point somewhere on the map.

After each child has had a turn, say: **There are Christians living in every country that you pointed to.** Ask:

● **Why do you think there are Christians in all of those countries?**

Have a child read aloud Mark 16:15. Then ask the children to repeat it. Say: **Jesus told his disciples to go into the world and preach the good news.** Ask:

● **What is this good news?**

● **What would have happened if the disciples had chosen not to obey Jesus?**

Say: **As the church grew, missionaries traveled all over the world to tell people about Jesus. Many people became Christians, and there are now Christian churches in those countries. To celebrate the fact that there are Christians all over the world, we're going to learn to say "Good news" today in three different languages: Portuguese, Danish, and French.**

Point to the countries on the globe as you teach each of these phrases to the children:

Portuguese: Boas Noticias (pronounced "Bo-as No-te-see-us")

Danish: Gode Nyheder (pronounced "Gude New-heaver")

French: Bonne Nouvelles (pronounced "Bun New-vell")

Ask the children to listen for ways the words sound like our English words and ways they sound different.

Have the children recite the Bible verse together. Then say: **And Christians went to Portugal to spread the good news.** Have the children go around the room shaking hands and saying, "Good news," to one another in Portuguese.

Repeat the activity, having the kids recite the verse and then greet each other in Danish. Repeat the activity again using the French words.

When finished, say the following prayer, asking children to fill in the languages when you pause: **Dear God, Jesus said, "Go into all the world and preach the good news to all creation." Thank you for this good news, or as they say in Portuguese, "Boas Noticias," as they say in Danish, "Gode Nyheder," and as they say in French, "Bonne Nouvelles." We pray in the name of Jesus. Amen.**

Invite children to enjoy the snack.

INTERPERSONAL

Partner Pass

> "Do to others as you would have them do to you."
>
> LUKE 6:31

SUPPLIES: You'll need a soft sponge ball.

Say: **The Bible tells us, "Do to others as you would have them do to you." We're going to learn Luke 6:31 as we do an activity together.**

Gather the whole group in a large circle. Tell the kids that they are to throw the sponge ball to someone in the circle in exactly the way they would like to have the ball returned to them. The person who receives the ball will pass the ball back in a like manner. The original holder will return the ball to you. The two children will then be seated. Before the first thrower begins, the group will remind the person with the Scripture verse, "Do to others as you would have them do to you."

Before the second thrower returns the ball, the group will say, "Luke 6:31." Kids will have fun using a warning tone of voice. Repeat the process until all the children have partners.

Then have the partners sit together. Ask the following questions and have partners discuss them. Let the first thrower answer first.

● **How do you think the two of you did following directions?** (Give a few seconds for the first partner to respond; then it's the second partner's turn.)

● **What are some reasons it might have been hard for the second person to return the ball in exactly the same way it was passed?**

● **What were you thinking when you threw the ball?**

● **Were you able to throw the ball in exactly the way you would have liked to? Why or why not?**

Have each pair join with another pair to form a foursome. Have foursomes discuss these questions. Ask:

● **What happens when you are kind to someone and they are not kind in return?** (Pause.)

● **Does it change how you want to be treated? Why or why not?**

Have the whole group join back together. When they are settled, ask:

● **Are there any advantages to treating people as you want to be treated?**

● **Can you think of any disadvantages?**

● **From the Scripture we are memorizing, what do you think Jesus would want us to do?**

Affirm all contributions, and then have all the children repeat Luke 6:31 together one more time.

Answers to *Search It Out:*

BODILY-KINESTHETIC

Action Reaction

> "So I say to you: Ask and it will be given to you; seek and you will find; knock and the door will be opened to you."
>
> LUKE 11:9

SUPPLIES: You'll need small candies and a scrumptious-looking treat such as iced brownies.

Before the children arrive, hide at least one piece of candy per child in your room. Put the iced brownies out of sight.

Tell children they'll have a candy treasure hunt—but first they must step outside the room and wait on the other side of the door. Once children are outside the room, explain these rules; then quickly shut the door so that the children are outside and you are inside. The rules are:

- They can't open the door. They must repeat the passwords before entering.
- Once they're inside, they must repeat the passwords before searching.

Wait a moment; then call through the closed door: **It looks like we're ready for a treasure hunt. All I need now are kids to play. I wish they'd say the passwords so I can open the door. Someone please give me the passwords.**

Someone will say they don't know the password. Crack open the door and say: **"So I say to you...Knock and the door will be opened to you."** Then shut the door again, and wait for the children to knock. Then swing the door wide open.

Ask children to repeat after you: **"So I say to you...Knock and the door will be opened to you."**

After children are in the room ask them to repeat after you before searching: **"Seek and you will find."** Then send them to search for the candy.

After the candy has been found, gather children around you at the front of the room. Then make a big production of bringing out the iced brownies. Say: **"Ask and it will be given to you."** Ask everyone to repeat that line after you, then give everyone a brownie. Ask:

- **During our treasure hunt, I asked you to do three things. What were they?**

Say: **Jesus says in the Gospel of Luke, "So I say to you: Ask and it will be given to you; seek and you will find; knock and the door will be opened to you." Let's repeat that several times together.**

Have the children repeat the verse with you. It might help to point to the brownies, the candy, and the door to help the children remember the order of the phrases.

Say: **This verse is about prayer. Let's talk about what this verse says about prayer.** Ask:

● **When Jesus said, "Ask and it will be given to you," what do you think he meant?**

● **What do you think we'll find when we seek?**

● **What will we find when the door has been opened to us?**

Say: **Jesus went on to say that God is our Father in heaven who will give us good gifts—the things we need. Jesus was saying in this verse that we can trust God to take care of us. That's a good thing to know. Let's say the verse again.**

Have the children say the verse again.

♫♫ MUSICAL

Hear and Obey Rap

> *"Blessed rather are those who hear the word of God and obey it."*
>
> **LUKE 11:28**

SUPPLIES: You'll need Bibles.

Read the verse aloud. Have kids repeat it with you; then help them put the verse to a rap rhythm. Congratulate them for creating the "Hear and Obey Rap."

Repeat the rap a few times, and then ask:

● **What are some things God's Word tells us to do?**

● **Tell about a time you obeyed God's Word. What good things happened as a result?**

Let kids respond, then say: **Luke 11:28 teaches that we'll be blessed if we obey God's Word. Let's take a few minutes to look at some specific rules in the Bible that God wants us to obey. You've probably heard them before—they're called the Ten Commandments.**

Form groups of four. Give each group a Bible and help them find and read the Ten Commandments in Exodus 20.

Say: **Choose one commandment you'll work on obeying this week. In your group, answer these questions about your commandment:**

● **What will you do this week to obey your commandment?**

● **What good things will happen as a result?**

Allow a few minutes for kids to select a commandment and discuss the questions. Then say: **To help us remember these commandments, we're going to turn them into verses for our "Hear and Obey Rap." Work with the others in your group to put your commandment to a rap rhythm. When you're done, we'll put all the verses and chorus together.**

Circulate among the groups and help kids work out rhythms for their commandments. Then call everyone back together, and have groups take turns leading the rest of the class in their commandment raps. It's OK if several children have chosen the same commandment. After all the groups have presented their raps, have everyone do the entire rap together, including the memory verse chorus.

Naturalistic

Fantastic Flowers

> *"Consider how the lilies grow. They do not labor or spin. Yet I tell you, not even Solomon in all his splendor was dressed like one of these."*
>
> LUKE 12:27

SUPPLIES: You'll need a Bible, plastic spoons, water, cotton balls, and flowers to plant. Plan ahead by asking children to wear play clothes. Ask for permission to plant flowers on the church grounds. You may want to bring garbage bags for kids who forget to wear play clothes. Cut a neck hole in the bottom of the bag and armholes in the sides of each bag.

Take your children outside to plant some flowers. Have the children sit in a circle around the plants. Use a spoon to carefully loosen the soil around the roots of one of the plants. Let children examine the roots. Explain how the plant takes in nourishment through its roots and leaves. Talk about how the blossom attracts bees and butterflies that carry the flower's pollen from one blossom to another to help the flowers make more flowers. Match the discussion to the understanding of your children.

Open your Bible to Luke 12:27. Ask one of the children to read the verse.

● **How did this flower grow?**

● **What exactly did it do to be so beautiful?**

Say: **This verse compares the beauty of a flower like this one to the splendor of a king dressed in all of his royal finery. But for us, the second sentence of this verse is hard to understand because we buy our clothes in the store. In Bible times, people were much more involved in making clothes: They even made the yarn and the thread that was woven into cloth and then sewn into clothes. The word "spin" in this verse means turning cotton or another material into thread. Let's practice spinning the way ancient people did it.**

Give each child a cotton ball. Real cotton works best. Have them pull apart the cotton into a large wispy square. Then have them pull and twist the cotton into a long piece of thread or yarn. Lead the children in saying the verse with you several times during this activity. Then ask:

● **Look at your clothes and see how tightly the threads are woven together. How long do you think we would have to spin to have enough thread to make a shirt or a pair of pants?**

Read the verse again and ask:

● **Why did Jesus compare flowers to spinning and Solomon's royal robes?**

Say: **Let's plant these flowers. While we're planting try to imagine what King Solomon must have looked like. Think of his fancy robes and the jewels in his golden crown. He must have been amazing in all his royal finery.**

Let children work for a few minutes planting the flowers. Lead the children in saying the verse together several times. After the flowers are planted ask children to sit in a circle again. Ask:

● **Why do you think Jesus wanted us to look at the flowers?**

Say: **Jesus knew we can look at creation to see some of what God is like. God gave the flowers roots and leaves to take in nourishment. He gave them beautiful flowers to attract the bees. The flowers don't work hard to provide for themselves—God takes care of them. Jesus wanted us to know we should trust in God to care for us just as God takes care of flowers and all the rest of his creation.**

Let children take time to water their flowers and say the verse one more time.

 **MUSICAL**

Seek and Save

> *"For the Son of Man came to seek and to save what was lost."*
>
> LUKE 19:10

SUPPLIES: You'll need a Bible, a cassette of praise music, a battery-operated cassette player, and a radio.

Before class, set the volume controls on the radio and cassette player so the radio plays slightly louder than the praise music. Children should be able to hear the praise music, but have trouble distinguishing the words.

Say: **I'm going to play some praise music. Listen carefully and tell me what the words are about.**

Turn on the radio and play the praise music cassette at the same time. Play both sources of music for about a minute.

Then stop the music and ask:

● **What words did you hear?**

● **Was it easy or hard to hear the praise music? Explain.**

● **How is this experience like or unlike following Jesus?**

Say: **Just as the words of the praise music were lost, it's easy for us to get lost and forget what's most important—following Jesus. But Luke 19:10 says "For the Son of Man came to seek and to save what was lost." Let's say that together.** Ask:

● **In what ways can people be lost?**

● **What do you think this verse means when it says Jesus will seek and save us?**

Say: **Let's play a game about Jesus seeking and saving the lost.**

Choose one child to be Jesus. Say: (Name of child) **will be Jesus. Jesus will carry the cassette player of praise music. The rest of you will hide and pretend to be lost people. Then Jesus will seek you. Jesus, when you find someone, stop the music. Then we'll all say the verse together. Then Jesus will start the music again. The newly found person will follow Jesus for the rest of the game as Jesus hunts for other lost people.**

Play the game several times.

Map Makers

> "I am the way and the truth and the life. No one comes to the Father except through me."
>
> JOHN 14:6

SUPPLIES: You'll need a Bible, paper, and pencils. You'll also need small treasures that will appeal to your kids, such as candy or stickers.

Give each child a piece of paper, a pencil, and a small treasure. Say: **Today, each of you will hide the small treasure I've given you. Then you'll create a treasure map that you'll give to one of your classmates to follow. The first thing to do is to think of a good place to hide your treasure.**

Give the children an area in which they can hide their treasures. If you're working in a small classroom, you may want to have the children hide their treasures one at a time while the others wait in the hall or keep their eyes closed.

When all the treasures are hidden, have the children draw treasure maps and write clues that will lead someone to the treasure.

You may want to take time to talk about what needs to go on the map, such as a clearly described starting place, an X to mark the spot, and so on.

When the maps are finished, have the children exchange maps and follow them to find the treasures.

Gather the children together and ask:

● **What is so exciting about treasures and treasure maps?**

● **You knew in advance what your treasure would be—was it still fun to follow the map? Why or why not?**

Say: **There's a verse in the Bible that's kind of like a treasure map. It's John 14:6. Let's read it.** Read John 14:6. Say:

● **The "I" in this verse refers to Jesus. In what way is Jesus like a treasure map?**

● **In what ways does a treasure map work as "the way and the truth and the life"?**

● **In what ways is Jesus "the way and the truth and the life"?**

● **What does the last part of the verse mean—that no man comes to the Father except through Jesus?**

Say: **Unless people know, love, and follow Jesus, they won't be able to be with God. Those people need to know the way to Jesus. Let's create new treasure maps that will show the way to God. Be sure to use the verse as part of your treasure map.**

Distribute more paper and pencils to the children. Periodically while the children are working, let your fingers "walk" on a child's map, and say the memory verse aloud with the class. Have the child explain what he or she is including in the map. Repeat until you have visited every child's map.

To close, have the children show their maps to each other and explain the way to God. Have the class respond to each child's map by repeating the verse aloud.

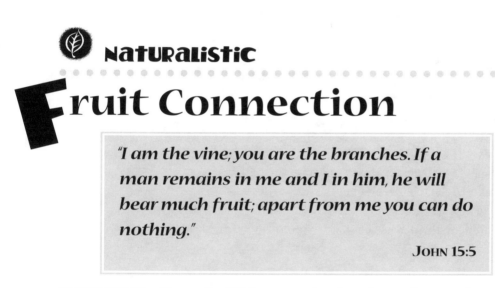

Naturalistic

Fruit Connection

> *"I am the vine; you are the branches. If a man remains in me and I in him, he will bear much fruit; apart from me you can do nothing."*
>
> JOHN 15:5

SUPPLIES: You'll need a Bible, some broken branches, and an apple for each child. You may also want a book that identifies the trees that are abundant in your area.

Have children gather in an orchard or wooded area, or even around a single tree in your church's yard. If you are able to meet in a wooded area, study the different kinds of trees around you. Have the children identify the trees. Young children can distinguish between conifer trees and deciduous trees. Older children may be able to tell you the difference among several varieties of conifers or deciduous trees.

Encourage each child to find a broken branch or twig on the ground, and then ask children to join you around a specific tree. Choose a tree with a dead limb or broken branch or find a large branch on the ground and hold it up.

Say: **God's Word compares the relationship between us and God to branches and vines. Jesus may have been talking about a grapevine and it's branches. But since we're here around this tree, let's pretend Jesus**

was talking about trees and tree branches. Open your Bible to John 15:5, and have a child read the passage aloud. Then have each child hold up the branch he or she found. Ask:

- **What will grow on the branches we're holding? Why?**
- **What would have to happen in order for these branches to grow fruit or leaves?**
- **What does it mean to be like a branch in God?**
- **What do we need to do to grow more like God?**
- **What things can we do to help us "remain in him?"**

Have children all hold their branches while you repeat the verse one phrase at a time. Encourage children to echo each phrase.

Phrase 1: I am the vine;

Phrase 2: you are the branches.

Phrase 3: If a man remains in me and I in him,

Phrase 4: he will bear much fruit;

Phrase 5: apart from me you can do nothing.

Before saying the verse again, give each child an apple and encourage the children to do these actions while echoing each phrase.

Phrase 1: Have them touch the trunk of a tree.

Phrase 2: Encourage children to shake a live branch.

Phrase 3: Let children touch where the branch connects to the tree.

Phrase 4: Instruct children to pick up their apples.

Phrase 5: Ask children to put the apples down.

Repeat at least twice, and then have the children enjoy their fruity snacks while continuing the discussion of how to remain in Christ.

So That You May Believe

> "But these are written that you may believe that Jesus is the Christ, the Son of God, and that by believing you may have life in his name."
>
> JOHN 20:31

SUPPLIES: You'll need Bibles, newsprint, tape, a marker, index cards, and pencils.

Write the memory verse on a sheet of newsprint, and post it on the wall. Have the children read it together. Say: **This verse comes almost at the very end of the Gospel of John. In this verse, John explains why he wrote the gospel. John wanted his readers to believe that Jesus was the Christ, the Son of God. And John wanted his readers to find eternal life as a result of reading this gospel.**

To help us learn this verse, we're going to pretend we're lawyers in a courtroom. It's our job to prove to the court that Jesus is the Christ, the Son of God. We're going to use the book of John as our evidence. It's your job to review John's book and find places where John showed how Jesus was special. These are the things I want you to look for:

● miracles Jesus performed;

● words that show Jesus was more than just a person;

● people Jesus met who thought he was important;

● places where John encourages his readers to put their faith in Jesus; and

● anything else that proves Jesus was the Christ, the Son of God.

Write each piece of evidence you find on an index card, and include the reference in John. For example, there's a sentence in the book of John that explains that Jesus is God's only begotten Son. For that piece of evidence you could write that Jesus is God's Son, and you would also write down John 3:16 because that's where the information is found.

Divide the book of John among the children. Some children will prefer to work in groups for this activity. Others may prefer to work alone.

Give the children five to ten minutes to work. Then say: **John wrote, "But these are written that you may believe that Jesus is the Christ, the Son of**

God, and that by believing you may have life in his name." Let's see what kind of evidence John used to prove his case.

Have the children each share their findings. Before each child shares, have the class recite the verse. After each child shares, ask:

● **How does this information help the reader believe in Jesus?**

After everyone has shared, end your activity by thanking God for sending his Son and thanking God for John, who wrote the Gospel of John, to help others believe in Jesus.

Public Relations for Jesus

> *"For we cannot help speaking about what we have seen and heard."*
>
> ACTS 4:20

SUPPLIES: You'll need a Bible, paper, pencils, a chalkboard and chalk or newsprint and a marker, and assorted office supplies.

Gather the children together. Say: **After Jesus went to heaven, Jesus' disciples went everywhere telling people about Jesus. Two of these disciples were Peter and John. The Jewish leaders didn't want Peter and John to teach others about Jesus, and the leaders tried to force Peter and John to stop. This verse from the book of Acts is how Peter and John answered the leaders.**

Read Acts 4:20 to the children. Then ask:

● **Why do you think the disciples couldn't stop speaking about what they had seen and heard?**

● **Have you ever been so excited about something that happened that you couldn't wait to tell someone about it? Explain.**

Say: **This is the way Peter, John, and the other disciples felt about what had happened to them. They had seen Jesus come back to life after he was crucified. And they had watched as Jesus rose up in the clouds to go back to heaven. It was big news!**

In Bible times, the only way to get the message out was for people like Peter and John to preach, give speeches, or to meet with people in

their homes and tell them. Today we have lots of different ways of telling people when important news happens. Ask:

● **In our society, how do we tell others about big news?**

Say: **We have newspapers, the radio, and television to help us spread big news. Some people are hired to find just the right way to spread important news. They are called public relations directors. Let's pretend all of you are public relations directors. You have to choose the best way to tell other people about Jesus. It might be a jingle people will hear on the radio. You might write a commercial for television, design an advertisement for a billboard, or write a press release for a newspaper. Decide how you will tell others about Jesus, and then write up your idea. You must include the verse somewhere in what you create.**

Give paper and pencils to the children and make markers, rulers, tape, poster board or other office supplies available to them. Write the words from Acts 4:20 on a chalkboard or newsprint so that the children will be able to use it in what they create. Give the children ten to fifteen minutes to create. Then gather the children together, and have each person read his or her idea to the rest of the class. After each child shares, have everyone read the verse together.

 **Naturalistic**

Signs of God

> "For since the creation of the world God's invisible qualities—his eternal power and divine nature—have been clearly seen, being understood from what has been made, so that men are without excuse."
>
> ROMANS 1:20

SUPPLIES: You'll need a Bible, index cards, and pencils.

Take kids to an outdoor area and have them spread out and sit down on the grass or a sidewalk. Be sure to bring a Bible with you. Have kids close their eyes and listen quietly for signs of life. They might hear their own breathing, birds chirping, footsteps or voices in the distance.

Let kids listen for one minute, and then have them open their eyes. Ask:

● **What signs of life did you hear?**

● **What sounds did you hear that you don't usually notice? Why don't you hear those sounds all the time?**

Say: **When we pay attention, we can see and hear signs of creation everywhere. God's Word says creation is a witness to his existence. Let's read what it says.**

Open your Bible to Romans 1:20, and ask a volunteer to read the verse aloud. Ask:

● **How does creation give witness to God?**

● **How did the sounds you heard give witness to God?**

Form groups of four. In each group, have one child take one section of the verse, dividing it in these phrases:

Phrase 1: For since the creation of the world God's invisible qualities—

Phrase 2: his eternal power and divine nature—have been clearly seen,

Phrase 3: being understood from what has been made,

Phrase 4: so that men are without excuse.

Have the children write their phrases down on index cards. In each group, have the children go around the circle and read their verse cards in order. Have the person in each group with the fourth phrase mention one thing from nature that show's God's power or shows God's divine nature. Have the children pass the cards one person to the right and do the activity again. Continue through several rounds. Have everyone say the entire verse together.

REFLECTIVE

n All Things

> *"And we know that in all things God works for the good of those who love him, who have been called according to his purpose."*
>
> ROMANS 8:28

SUPPLIES: You'll need a Bible, paper, pencils, and chalkboard and chalk or newsprint and a marker.

Give each child a sheet of paper and a pencil. If you have nonwriters in your group, pair them with writers, or do this activity verbally as a group.

Say: **Let's begin this activity by writing down all the terrible, awful things that might happen to someone your age. Some of them can be serious things that could really happen. For example, you could fall through the ice when you're skating at the park. And some of them can be silly things that would probably never happen. For example, a meteorite might crash into your bedroom. Use your imagination, and think up at least fifteen terrible things that could happen to you.**

Give the children about five minutes to write a list of terrible things that might happen. While the children are working, write the memory verse on a chalkboard or newsprint. When the time is up, have volunteers read items from their lists to the rest of the class.

Say: **It doesn't matter who you are or where you live. At some point, something bad or painful is going to happen to you. It's just as true that good and pleasant things will happen to everybody at some time. But God has promised us that no matter what happens he'll be working in our lives. This verse tells us what God will do with the circumstances of our lives. Let's read the verse together.** Read Romans 8:28 aloud with the children. Ask:

- **How can this verse be true?**
- **In what ways does God work for good?**
- **Who are the people this verse talks about?**

Say: **Let's say the verse together again. Recite the verse with the children. Now I'd like you to use your imagination again to consider and ponder how God might turn your terrible awful situations into good. For example, if the meteorite crashes into your bedroom, you might learn more about the stars and become an important astronomer.**

Give the children several minutes to consider how God might work for good in the midst of bad circumstances. Then have the children each share their thoughts with the rest of the class by reading aloud their bad circumstances, reciting the verse, and then reading aloud how God might work in the circumstance.

Close in prayer, thanking God for being in control of every circumstance and for taking care of us by working for our good.

☺ InterPersonal

The Twelve-Thirteen Plan

> *"Share with God's people who are in need. Practice hospitality."*
>
> **ROMANS 12:13**

SUPPLIES: You'll need a Bible, newsprint, a marker, paper, and pencils.

Interpersonal learners are "party hearty" people: They may want to plan more than is possible. However, this activity is very flexible. You can use it to plan a party for your own class, for another class or group within the church, or as a service project for a group outside your church.

It's important that the kids carry out their plans. It's probable that this activity will take more than one session to complete. Before starting the planning process, decide on the limits of your group's ability to offer hospitality. Be ready to gently rein the kids in and scale back the event if necessary.

Gather the children together, and say: **Romans 12:13 tells us to "share with God's people who are in need.** Practice hospitality." Ask:

● **What are some ways our group could practice hospitality?** List the children's ideas on a sheet of newsprint.

Say: **Let's think about God's people who are in need.** Ask:

● **Who do you know that is needy?** List these in a separate place on the newsprint.

Say: **Is there any way we could do something from the hospitable list that would allow us to share with God's people who are in need?** Form groups of three or four, and have groups discuss your question. After about two minutes, ask for reports from each group. Be prepared for some really creative suggestions. After each group reports its ideas, have the whole class repeat the verse.

Then as a class, evaluate which ideas are possible for your group to do. For example, on a small scale, you might decide your group could bake cookies to serve to the church staff. On a large scale, you might invite the whole church to a party and ask each person to bring an item that would benefit one of the "people in need" you have listed. Whatever you decide to do, call it the "Twelve-Thirteen Plan" as a way to reinforce Romans 12:13.

List the things your group would need to consider to pull off the "Twelve-Thirteen Plan," such as food, games, decoration, and delivery. Form committees according to these categories. Assign each child to one of the committees, and have each committee appoint a leader (who will keep the committee on task), a recorder (who will write things down) and a reporter (who will inform the rest of the group.) Help each committee develop its plans, offering guidance as necessary.

As the children on a particular committee make a final decision about something, have them stand and call out, "Twelve-Thirteen!" The rest of the children will respond by jumping up and saying the verse together with the reference. After the committees have finished planning (or after a predetermined time), gather all the children together, and have the reporters tell the whole group what they've decided.

Be sure to have the children carry out their plans as soon as possible.

✋ BODILY-KINESTHETIC

Two Things at Once

> "So whether you eat or drink or whatever you do, do it all for the glory of God."
>
> 1 CORINTHIANS 10:31

SUPPLIES: You'll need Bibles and crackers. You may also want to have a vacuum cleaner handy.

Say: **Sometimes it's hard to do two things at once. For example, it takes a little bit of practice to rub your belly and pat your head all at the same time. Let's try it.**

Have the children rub their bellies and pat their heads.

Say: **That's pretty hard. Some people can do it, and some people never can get the hang of it. For some people, it's even hard to chew gum and walk at the same time. Some things are tough to do when you're already doing something else. I've got another tough one for us to try. Let's see if any of us can eat a cracker and whistle at the same time.**

Hand out crackers to anyone who wants to try. Have volunteers chew up a cracker and then try to whistle before they've swallowed the cracker. This is great fun because the children won't be able to whistle without blowing cracker crumbs out of their mouths. Children may be a little reluctant at first, but as soon as one child has tried it, most of the other children will be eager to have a turn.

Say: **That was a lot of fun! It's next to impossible to whistle with cracker crumbs in your mouth. But there are other things we do all at the same time without even thinking about it. For example, no matter what you're doing, your heart is beating. There are a few people who have great control over their bodies. These people can slow their heart rate, but their hearts never stop. Let's see if we can do it.**

Have everyone try to slow their heartbeats down. Then ask:

● **How did that go? Could you slow down your heart?**

Say: **Here's another one. No matter what, you can't go for more than a minute or so without breathing. We never have to remind ourselves to breathe—it just happens no matter what else we're doing. There's a verse in the Bible that talks about doing more than one thing at the same time. Let's read it together.** Distribute Bibles. Have the children look up 1 Corinthians 10:31, and read it together. Ask:

● **What do you think this verse means?**

● **How can we glorify God when we're doing such basic things as eating and drinking?**

● **Is it really possible to glorify God no matter what we're doing? How?**

● **Why does God want us to glorify him all the time?**

Say: **Let's practice the verse. Each of us will have a chance to think of something we do in the course of our lives. Next we'll all act it out and then say the verse together.**

Have children each think of an action such as brushing their teeth, waiting for the bus, doing their homework, or playing a part in the school play. Let the entire class act it out. Then have everyone recite the verse together. Before going on to the next child's suggestion, ask:

● **How can you glorify God while you're doing that?**

You might want to vacuum the cracker crumbs from the floor after this activity.

÷≠ Logical-Mathematical

Different and the Same

> *"There are different kinds of service, but the same Lord."*
>
> 1 CORINTHIANS 12:5

SUPPLIES: You'll need a Bible, newsprint, a marker, tape, paper, and pencils.

Tape two sheets of newsprint on the wall. On one sheet of newsprint, write the memory verse. On the other sheet of newsprint, write the word "Lord" in a small space in the center of the newsprint. Refer to the margin illustration if you're unsure about what a mind web looks like.

Say: **Today we're going to explore this verse.** Read the verse aloud with the children. **We're going to do a mind web. I'd like you to consider different ways to serve God. We'll brainstorm for a while and I'll write your ideas on the newsprint in a web form.** Ask:

● **What are some different ways in which we can serve God?**

Write down the children's ideas in a similar format to the margin illustration. After several minutes of brainstorming, say: **There are different kinds of service** (point to the webbed ideas)**, but the same Lord.** (Point to the word "Lord.") Ask:

● **Why is it important to remember that all Christians, no matter what they do, serve the same God?**

Say: **Later on in this chapter from 1 Corinthians, Paul gives a word picture to help us understand how there are different kinds of service but the same Lord. Paul says the Church is one unit made up of many parts that all work together. Paul says that unit is like a person's body. Jesus is the head or the brain of the body, and the body parts, like hands, feet, eyes, and ears, all do their own jobs, but they work together under the leadership of the brain.**

Let's see if we can come up with other word pictures of how this 1 Corinthians 12:5 works. Think of something that has many parts, but that all works together. Draw a diagram or write a description of your idea. Be sure to include the memory verse in your diagram.

Hand out paper and pencils and give the children five to ten minutes to work. They may come up with ideas such as

● a car (the engine is God, the body is the Church, and the wheels are the different kinds of service), or

● an imaginary machine with various cogs, gears, and conveyor belts that show the different kinds of service.

After several minutes, have the children share their ideas and models with the class, and explain how they illustrate the verse. Have the class repeat the verse after each child shares.

InterPersonaL

Bumper Cars

> "Love is patient, love is kind. It does not envy, it does not boast, it is not proud."
>
> 1 CORINTHIANS 13:4

SUPPLIES: You'll need a Bible, newsprint, a marker, paper plates, and masking tape. Before the activity begins, use the masking tape to lay down a large Tick-Tack-Toe style grid. Fill as much of the room as possible with the grid.

Write the verse on the newsprint, and post it on the wall where the children can see it. Have the children sit in a circle. Say: **First Corinthians 13:4 tells us that "love is patient, love is kind. It does not envy, it does not boast, it is not proud."**

Point to the first part of the verse, and say: **Turn to your neighbor, and tell him or her about one time you were able to show love by being patient.**

Point to the next section of the verse, and say: **Now tell your partner about a time you saw someone show love by being kind.**

Point to the next section of the verse, and say: **Tell your neighbor about a time you were tempted to envy someone for something they had but you didn't.**

Point to the next section of the verse, and say: **Tell your neighbor about a time when you wanted to boast or brag.**

Point to the last section of the verse, and say: **The word "proud" here means that you consider yourself to be more important than others. This phrase** means that when we love others, we consider them to be more important than we are. Tell your neighbor about a time when you saw someone who considered others to be more important than himself or herself.

Say: **Grown-ups sometimes get to practice these loving attitudes when they drive! Today, we're going to see if it works for kids, too!**

Have kids form "cars" of two, three, or four. The two passengers in the front seat can link arms. The passengers in the back seat can link arms, and each put his or her other arm on the shoulder of the passenger in front. Have each "car" choose a masking-tape street to start on. Determine a signal that will mean, "All cars brake!" Give each driver a paper plate to be a steering wheel.

On your cue, the cars will all begin to travel. Each car needs to say "vroom-vroom" or "putt-putt" (or other car sounds) together as it travels. The driver can decide to take any turns he or she wants, based on input from the passengers. When the cars find themselves heading for other cars, they must brake. The first to stop begins the verse: "Love is patient," the other car responds, "Love is kind." They alternate phrases of the verse, ending with the Scripture reference.

When the verse is complete, each car rotates position of the passengers in a clockwise manner, and play continues. To add interest to the game, the teacher can change the speed limits at which the cars are allowed to operate.

Have the children all say the entire verse whenever you give the signal that means, "All cars brake!"

Conclude the activity by having all cars say the verse in unison.

BODiLY-KineStHetic

Guard Duty

> *"Be on your guard; stand firm in the faith; be men of courage; be strong."*
>
> 1 CORINTHIANS 16:13

Supplies: You'll need a Bible.

Ask your children to form a large circle with you. Say: **It's time to be soldiers! We're going to do four things that soldiers do. On my signal, march to your right until I stop. Then do as I do, and say what I say. Company, march!**

Have the children follow as you march around the circle several times.

Then say: **Company, halt!** and stand stiffly at attention, heels together. Say: **Repeat after me: "Be on your guard!"**

Ask children to repeat the phrase twice, and then march around the circle once.

Spread your feet and stand as if you're going to be attacked. Say: **Repeat after me: "Stand firm in the faith!"**

Ask children to repeat the phrase twice, and then march around the circle once.

Point proudly to your heart, and say: **Repeat after me: "Be men of courage!"**

Ask children to repeat the phrase twice, and then march around the circle once.

Flex your biceps, and say: **Repeat after me: "Be strong!"** Ask children to repeat the phrase twice.

March children around the circle once, and then pause and have them do all four actions in order. Lead them in the actions and the verse at least twice: **"Be on your guard; stand firm in the faith; be men of courage; be strong."**

Gather children together and sum up: **These four things that soldiers do are things the Apostle Paul says we should do as followers of Jesus.**

- **What's something you should be on guard for as a Christian?**
- **What's one way you can stand firm in your faith this week?**
- **How can you have courage when you're living as a Christian?**
- **What's a way you can be strong in your Christian faith?**

Close by repeating the verse and the actions several more times.

⌗ Logical-Mathematical

Living Through Me

> *"I have been crucified with Christ and I no longer live, but Christ lives in me."*
>
> **GALATIANS 2:20**

SUPPLIES: You'll need a Bible, newsprint, and a marker.

Say: Today we'll be learning Galatians 2:20. Read Galatians 2:20. Say: **This verse talks about what happens when we become Christians. Let's think about this verse a bit. The first part of this verse says, "I have been crucified with Christ."** Ask:

- **What do you think this means?**

● **In what ways have you died or been crucified?**

Say: **The next part of the verse says, "and I no longer live." Ask:**

● **What do you think this means?**

● **If we no longer live, then why do we still make plans for ourselves? why do we still sin and make mistakes?**

Say: **The last part of the verse says, "but Christ lives in me."**

● **What do you think this means?**

● **In what ways does Christ live in you?**

Post a sheet of newsprint on the wall and draw a figure of a person on the newsprint. (Refer to the margin illustration.)

Point to the hands, and say: **"I have been crucified with Christ and I no longer live, but Christ lives in me." Ask:**

● **If Christ lives in me, what do my hands do?**

Write the children's answers next to the newsprint figure's hands.

Then point to the figure's feet, and have the class recite the verse with you. Ask:

● **If Christ lives in me, where do my feet go?**

Write the children's answers next to the newsprint figure's feet.

Point to the figure's eyes, and have the children recite the verse. Ask:

● **If Christ lives in me, what do my eyes see?**

Write the children's answers next to the newsprint figure's eyes.

Point to the figures mouth, and have the class recite the verse with you. Ask:

● **If Christ lives in me, what do I say?**

Write the children's answers next to the newsprint figure's mouth.

Point to the figure's head, and have the class recite the verse with you. Ask:

● **If Christ lives in me, how do I think?**

Write the children's answers next to the newsprint figure's head.

Point to the figure's heart, and have the class recite the verse with you. Ask:

● **If Christ lives in me, how does that affect how I feel?**

Write the children's answers next to the newsprint figure's heart.

Say: **Consider all that we've talked about and review what we've written on this newsprint. Choose one or two things from this list you'd like to have as a part of your life—something that will show that Christ lives in you.**

Give the children a moment to review the newsprint. Then pray: **Lord Jesus, we thank you for the sacrifice you made for us when you died for our sins. Jesus, we have learned that when we become a Christian, you live within us. We no longer live for our own purposes, but we live to please you. Please help us to live lives that show your presence and your priorities. Thank you. Amen.**

Spirit Fruit

> *"The fruit of the Spirit is love, joy, peace, patience, kindness, goodness, faithfulness, gentleness, and self-control."*
>
> GALATIANS 5:22-23

SUPPLIES: You'll need Bibles, newsprint, tape, markers, index cards, pencils, and several concordances.

Before the children arrive, tape the newsprint to the wall to create a large mural. On the mural draw a tree with roots. (Refer to the margin illustration.) Also draw nine pieces of fruit in the tree, and write one of the fruits of the spirit on each piece of fruit. At the top of the mural, write the verse.

Gather the children and say: **Today we're going to learn a verse about fruit. To do that we'll think like orchard farmers. Sometimes orchards produce good crops, and sometimes orchards produce bad crops.** Have the children refer to what you've drawn below ground and above ground to answer the following questions. Ask:

● **What conditions affect the crop above ground and below ground?**

● **If we want our orchard to grow the crops I have written on the pieces of fruit, what would the conditions need to be like in our lives?**

Say: **A crop is the result of the farmer's work plus the state of the environment. Let's do some investigating about what the Bible says about these fruits and how to grow a good crop of them.**

Hand out the index cards and pencils. Form as many groups as you have concordances. Divide up the fruits of the Spirit among the groups. Have each group look up their "fruits" in the concordance and then look up the verses in the Bible to see what the Bible teaches about developing the fruits of the Spirit. Then have the children write on the cards what they learn about growing a good crop of spiritual fruit.

Give the children several minutes to work. Periodically get the children's attention and call out, "And the fruit of the Spirit is…" and have the groups call out in the order of Galatians 5:22-23 the fruits they've been assigned. For example, if Group 1 has been assigned "love" and "joy" and Group 2 has been assigned "patience" and "kindness," Group 1 will call out its words, and then Group 2 will call out its words.

After several minutes of work, have each group report to the entire class what they've learned. Let groups post their cards on the mural next to their group's fruits. After each group reports, have the entire class recite the verse.

interpersonal

Oops!

> *"Be kind and compassionate to one another, forgiving each other, just as in Christ God forgave you."*
>
> **EPHESIANS 4:32**

SUPPLIES: You'll need a Bible, cookies, and a chalkboard and chalk or newsprint and a marker.

Write the verse on a chalkboard or newsprint.

Say: **The name of the game we are playing today is Oops! To play, we will have to all have the attitude Paul tells us to have in Ephesians 4:32. We will need to "be kind and compassionate to one another, forgiving each other, just as in Christ God forgave you."** Gather kids together in groups of no more than ten, and have them stand shoulder to shoulder.

Any one of you can start by saying the first word of the verse. The idea is to get all the way to the end of the verse one word at a time, but no one can say two words in a row, and no two people can say a word at the same time. We have to say the reference at the end, too. If two people speak at the same time, we'll all say "Oops!" and we'll quote the whole verse together. Then we will begin again from the first word. The keys to success in this game are listening closely, and of course, being kind, compassionate and forgiving!

It will probably take a number of times around to get the whole verse right, so be ready to celebrate your success with some cookies! Some interpersonal learners are very good at anticipating others' behavior. Others will have a hard time waiting for another to speak when they know the word coming up. Either way, it's great practice for the give and take of relationships!

InterPersonal

Imitators

> "Be imitators of God, therefore, as dearly loved children."
>
> EPHESIANS 5:1

SUPPLIES: You'll need a Bible.

Say: Today we're going to do an activity about parents and children and how they relate to each other. Have you ever noticed how very young children like to imitate grown-ups? In fact, many of the things that little kids play with are toy versions of the things adults use every day. Ask:

● **What toys are versions of things adults use every day?**

Form two groups: the Parents and the Children. Say: **Now let's act out how little kids play. Let's form pairs so that each Parent is paired with a Child.**

Say: **Parents, I want you to act out something that parents do, such as driving a car or washing windows. Children, it's your job to imitate the Parents exactly.**

Give the kids a few minutes to follow your instructions. Then ask:

● **What was tough about being a good imitator?**

● **Children, what did you have to do to be a good imitator?**

● **Parents, did you do anything to help the Children be good imitators?**

● **Why do you think little kids like to imitate their parents?**

Say: **One reason children imitate their parents may be that children think their parents are special and important people. Children want to be like their parents, so they imitate their actions. There's a verse in the Bible that talks about this.** Read Ephesians 5:1, and then ask:

● **In what ways should we imitate God?**

● **Why is it important to imitate God?**

● **What did you learn from our activity that you can apply to the relationship between you and God?**

Say: **Let's try another activity now. Stay with your partner and sit cross-legged with your knees touching. If you were the Parent before, now you'll be the Imitator. If you were the Child, this time you'll be Leader who makes up the actions. Leaders, lead your partners in doing several actions. Imitators, copy everything your partners do, as if you** were mirrors reflecting each action. **Each time I clap my hands, we'll all say the verse together.**

Have the children do the activity for a couple of minutes. At least five times during the activity, clap your hands, and have the children say the verse together. Then have the children switch roles and repeat the activity.

 **LINGUISTIC**

House Rules Board Game

> *"Children, obey your parents in the Lord, for this is right."*
>
> EPHESIANS 6:1

SUPPLIES: Each child will need a small paper cup, a sheet of white construction paper, and a pencil or a fine point marker. You'll also need a chalkboard and chalk or newsprint and a marker, glue sticks, a large bag of M&M's candies, a bowl, and several sheets of yellow, red, green, brown and orange construction paper. Cut each colored sheet into twenty-four 2x2¼-inch pieces. Each child will need one square of blue paper and three squares of each other color.

Write the memory verse for all to see on a chalkboard or on newsprint. Read the verse with the group, and then say: **Even in Bible times, people talked about children obeying their parents because it is important for us to respect authority. However, not all families have exactly the same rules or the same chores.** Ask:

● **What rule do you have at your house that you think everyone else has, too?**

● **What chore do you do at your house that no one else has to do?**

Say: **Today you each will create your own board game about the house rules in your family.**

Give each child a pencil or marker and three paper squares in each of these colors: yellow, green, brown, and orange. Instruct children to write one rule (such as no running in the house) or one chore (such as setting the table) on each piece of paper. Help younger children with their printing, or suggest that they use symbols (such as a foot or a dish) to represent the rule or the chore. Next, give each child three squares of red paper. On each of the red squares, have the children write the word "disobey" and put a frowning face. Finally give each child one square of blue paper and ask them to draw a smiley face on it.

Give each child a sheet of white paper. The next step is to have each child place his or her paper pieces around the outside edges of a sheet of white paper, then use a glue stick to fasten each square to the paper. The children can also write the memory verse in the center of the board game.

Now it's time to play! Divide the M&M's candies into colors. Give each child a paper cup with several red, yellow, brown, orange, and green candies. Also give each child a blue M&M as a player piece.

Tell children to put the blue M&M on the blue square. Then have the children cover their cups with their hands and shake the M&M's. Then, without peeking, have the children each reach in his or her cup and pull out an M&M. Each child will move his or her blue M&M playing piece to the right to find the nearest square that is the same color as the M&M selected from the cup. If the children land on yellow, brown, green or orange squares, have them each read the chore or rule, eat the M&M candy, and say the memory verse before shaking the cup again. If they land on red squares, have them each put the red M&M aside and say, "Oh no, I should have obeyed."

Continue the process until children have gone around their boards one time. Children might enjoy switching game boards and playing again.

After the game, ask:

● **What rewards did you get for doing your chores and following the rules in this game?**

● **What rewards and benefits do you get for obeying in real life?**

● **What happened when you didn't obey?**

● **What happens in real life when you don't obey?**

● **Why is it important to obey our parents? Let's see how many different reasons we can think of.**

Say: **God has given us parents who have more knowledge and experience we do. Obeying our parents helps us to grow wise and it helps us learn how to obey God. Let's say the verse one more time together. Ready? "Children, obey your parents in the Lord, for this is right" (Ephesians 6:1).**

Strong in God

> *"Finally, be strong in the Lord and in his mighty power."*
>
> EPHESIANS 6:10

SUPPLIES: You'll need a Bible, a chalkboard and chalk or newsprint and a marker, paper, and markers or crayons.

Write Ephesians 6:10 on the chalkboard or newsprint, and have the children read it with you several times. Emphasize the words "strong" and "power" with your voice by making a fist or by flexing the muscles in your arm. Encourage the children to say the verse with the same emphasis that you use. Ask:

- **What do you think this verse means?**
- **How would being strong in the Lord affect your life?**
- **How do you become strong in the Lord?**

Hand out paper and markers or crayons. Say: **The Apostle Paul wrote the book of Ephesians. Right after this verse, Paul writes a description of what a person who is strong in the Lord looks like. Before we look at what Paul wrote, I'd like to know what you think being strong in the Lord looks like. You might think that it looks like a mighty mountain. Or you might think that it looks like a powerful bulldozer. Take a few minutes to draw a picture about what it looks like to be strong in the Lord and in his mighty power. Be sure to write the verse on your paper as a reminder of what you're drawing, and be ready to explain what you've drawn and how it relates to the verse.**

Give the children several minutes to draw their pictures. When everyone is finished, have each child show his or her drawing to the rest of the class. Lead the class in reciting the verse together; then have the child complete this sentence, "Being strong in the Lord is like _____ because_____." Continue until each child has shared his or her drawing with the rest of the class.

Then say: **You all chose wonderful visual images of being strong. The Apostle Paul said that being strong in the Lord is like a soldier who wears armor. The soldier is prepared to fight a mighty battle. Each piece of armor stands for a tool from God that helps the soldier win the fight. Let's pretend that we're wearing God's armor. Close your eyes and imagine** yourself wearing a belt of truth and a breastplate of right living. You're also wearing a shield of faith, a helmet of salvation, and the sword of God's Word. You are truly strong in the Lord. Let's say the verse together one more time. Recite the verse with the children.

REFLECTIVE

A Jesus Attitude

> *"Your attitude should be the same as that of Christ Jesus."*
>
> **PHILIPPIANS 2:5**

SUPPLIES: You'll need a Bible, a chalkboard and chalk or newsprint and a marker, pencils, and paper.

Write out the words from Philippians 2:5 on a chalkboard or newsprint. Give each child a sheet of paper and a pencil.

Say: **Say the words of Philippians 2:5 to yourself several times. You can refer to the verse as it is written on the chalkboard if you want. Think about this verse. Then write the word, "attitude" down the side of the paper. For each letter of the word, think about and write a word or short phrase that begins with that letter and names an attitude or quality about Jesus. For example, you might write: A—answers prayer, T—treasure, T—teacher, I—innocent, T—tested, U—understanding, D—dear Son, E—eternal.**

Give the children a few minutes to work. Periodically regain their attention, and have the class recite the verse together.

Then say: **Now consider why it's important to have the same attitude as Jesus. Next to the attitudes of Jesus, write down an attitude or character trait that you have. For example, you might write: A—athletic, T—trustworthy, T—talented, I—intelligent, T—terrific sense of humor, U—understanding, D—dynamic, E—excellent piano player.**

Give the children a few minutes to think and write. Periodically regain their attention, and have the class recite the verse together.

Gather the children together to compare and contrast Jesus' attitudes and traits with their own attitudes and traits. Then ask:

● **Why is it important to have an attitude like that of Jesus?**

● **What attitudes do you have that are like that of Christ Jesus?**

- **What attitudes could you change so that you can be more like him?**
- **Why is it sometimes difficult to have an attitude the same as that of Christ Jesus'?**
- **What steps could you personally take to have an attitude more like that of Jesus?**

Give kids time to reflect on these questions before answering. Close by reciting the verse together as a group.

❖ REFLECTIVE

Good Thoughts

> *"Finally, brothers, whatever is true, whatever is noble, whatever is right, whatever is pure, whatever is lovely, whatever is admirable—if anything is excellent or praiseworthy—think about such things."*
>
> **PHILIPPIANS 4:8**

SUPPLIES: You'll need a Bible, a chalkboard and chalk or newsprint and a marker, paper, and pencils.

Write the verse on the chalkboard or newsprint. Gather the children and read the verse aloud together. Ask:

- **Is this verse a suggestion or a command for Christians? Explain.**
- **Why do you think Scripture tells us to think on these things?**
- **What do you think will result from our thinking on these things?**

Hand out paper and pencils, and say: **As Christians, God wants to develop Christlike character in us. That means that as we grow, we take on traits that please God. For example, when we think on true things as this verse suggests, we begin to value things that are true, and we begin to develop a truthful character. To understand this we're going to look at this verse in an unusual way.**

When we study a Bible verse like this, sometimes it's helpful to consider what would happen if we did the opposite of what it says. The first thing I'd like you to do is to list all of the things that this verse tells us to do. Then consider each item on the list, and think of it's opposite. For

example, the opposite of true is false. Write down a second list that consists of all the opposites.

Then, consider what a person who always thinks about the first list would be like. Next, consider what a person who thinks on the second list would be like.

Give the children a few minutes to create and reflect on their lists. Then have volunteers share their character descriptions with the class.

Say: **Now let's think about what things are included in the good list. For example, what true things can you think of? What noble things can you think of? and so on. Create a new list on your papers.**

Give the children a few minutes to create the third list. Then have volunteers share their ideas with the class.

Say: **Now let's come up with a system to help us remember this verse. It will help us remember good things to think about. Let's write down the first letter of each thing the verse tells us to think about. Then we'll write sentences that have words that begin with each of those letters.**

Write down "TNRPLA" on the chalkboard, and have the children construct mnemonic sentences in which each word begins with one of the letters you've written on the board—for example, **T**en **N**ew **R**abbits **P**ushed **L**arry **A**side. The sillier the mnemonic, the easier it will be for kids to remember the order of items in the verse. Come up with as many mnemonics as possible. For each mnemonic, point to the first letter of each word and ask:

● **What does this letter remind you to think about?**

End this activity by saying the entire verse together.

Parade of Strength

> *"I can do everything through him who gives me strength."*
>
> **PHILIPPIANS 4:13**

SUPPLIES: You'll need a Bible, a CD or cassette player, a recording of a march or other upbeat instrumental music, scissors, and crepe paper streamers.

Before class, cut crepe paper streamers into three-foot lengths. Arrange to lead children on a parade route through your church.

Set out the pile of streamers. Ask:

● **What are some things that are hard for you to do?**

● **Who helps you do those things?**

Let kids respond, then say: **The Bible says that we can do anything with Jesus' help. Listen as I read Philippians 4:13.**

Read the verse, and then have kids repeat it with you. Say: **Jesus gives us the strength to stand up to people who pick on us, be nice to people who are different than we are, and forgive people who are mean to us. He can help us do anything. Today we're going to celebrate that with a parade.**

Give each child two streamers. Say: **When we march in our parade, we'll wave streamers. Let's listen to some parade music and practice waving our streamers now. When the music is soft, wave your streamers in front of you slowly. When the music gets louder and stronger, wave your streamers over your head quickly.**

Play the march music, and let kids practice waving streamers. After you practice with the music several times, say: **That's great! Our parade will be very festive with the music and streamers. But we want people to know why we're celebrating. So let's sing our memory verse along with the music.**

Help children sing the words of the verse along with the melody. Don't forget to include the verse reference! Children will probably fit the verse to the music easily since they've already heard the melody several times. When you're ready for your parade, set the CD or cassette player in your doorway (or carry it with you if it's battery-operated) and lead children along your planned route.

interpersonal

Bear and Share

> *"Bear with each other and forgive whatever grievances you may have against one another. Forgive as the Lord forgave you."*
>
> COLOSSIANS 3:13

SUPPLIES: You'll need a Bible.

Form pairs. Say: **Colossians 3:13 tells us to "bear with each other and forgive whatever grievances you may have against one another. Forgive as the Lord forgave you." There are a couple of words in this verse that we don't use very often. The first word is "bear." We don't often use the word "bear" in the same context as this verse. The word "bear" means to put up with. The other word is "grievance." It's kind of a big word that we don't say much. It means "complaints."**

Your job will be to work with your partner to come up with a presentation that illustrates this verse. Your presentation could include a cheer, a song, a poem, a skit, a rap, or anything else you want. The only rule is that your presentation must tell the rest of us what the verse means and how to obey the verse.

Give the children ten minutes to work on their presentations. Then have each pair give its presentation to the rest of the class. After each group has given its presentation, have the entire class repeat the verse. When all the groups have finished, ask:

● **Why do you think God wants us to bear with each other?**

● **How do you bear with each other at home? at school? at church?**

● **Did any of you have to bear with each other and forgive as you were working on your presentations? How did you resolve your conflicts?**

● **Why is it important for us to forgive each other?**

● **What's the difference between bearing with each other and forgiving each other?**

Say: **As Christians we are part of God's family. All families have disagreements and conflicts. Whenever people are together, you can count on the fact that sooner or later they will do things to annoy each other. But God wants us to learn how to live peacefully. God asks us to bear with each other—to have patience with others. And God wants us to be forgiving when others wrong us. God is pleased when we live graciously with each other.**

Work, Work, Work

> *"Whatever you do, work at it with all your heart, as working for the Lord, not for men."*
>
> COLOSSIANS 3:23

SUPPLIES: You'll need a box of flat toothpicks. Each box of five hundred toothpicks is enough for twenty-four children.

Form pairs. Give each pair about forty toothpicks.

Say: **Think of a person you don't like very much. It must be a person nobody else in our room knows! Maybe it's your Aunt Zelda who always pinches your cheek and kisses you at family reunions. Or maybe it's a boy who used to punch you at a school you attended before moving here. Think of that person, and tell your partner about him or her. Both partners please take a turn.**

When pairs have finished sharing, say: **Let's suppose those people you don't like ask you for a favor. They want you to build a fence with your toothpicks. They don't plan to pay you any money. They may not even thank you. Let's see how hard you'd work. In your pairs, take two minutes to build your fence.**

When two minutes have passed ask:

● **How hard did you work?**

● **Why didn't you work very hard?** or **Why did you work hard for someone you don't like?**

After children answer, say: **Now let's suppose Jesus asks you to build a fence. Take two minutes, and let's see how hard you'd work if Jesus asked you to do the job.**

When two minutes have passed, ask:

● **Did you approach building the fence with a different attitude this time? Why or Why not?**

When children have answered, gather up the toothpicks, and say: **Most of us work hard when we're being paid money or when we like the people we're working for. But the Apostle Paul says, "whatever you do, work at it with all your heart, as working for the Lord, not for men." Let's say the verse together.**

Repeat the verse a couple of times together; then say: **Let's repeat that verse again; when we get to the word "men," substitute the person you mentioned at the beginning of this activity—the one you don't like much.**

Repeat the verse together again. Then ask:

● **What's a job or chore you really hate doing? Do you do it well? Explain.**

● **How does this verse change your attitude toward work?**

● **What would change if you did chores as if you were working for the Lord?**

Ask children to turn to a partner and share one job or chore they'll do as if for the Lord this week.

Close by reciting the verse together several times.

 **LinGUistiC**

Letters of Love

> *"Therefore encourage one another and build each other up, just as in fact you are doing."*
>
> **1 THESSALONIANS 5:11**

SUPPLIES: You'll need a Bible, a chalkboard and chalk or newsprint and a marker, lined 8½x11-inch paper, a large envelope, markers or pens, and Christian stickers.

In this activity, children will write letters to send to children at another church. Obtain the address of a church that is far away from your church, perhaps even in another country. Your denominational office will be able to help you find a church, or perhaps your pastor or someone in your congregation knows a church with whom you can correspond. Prepare a cover letter to accompany the children's letters. In the cover letter, introduce your class, and explain that you're memorizing 1 Thessalonians 5:11 and that your class is putting the verse into action.

Gather the children together and ask:

● **Have you ever received a letter? Who did it come from?**

● **What's it like to get a letter?**

● **Do you write letters to other people? Who do you send your letters to?**

Then say: **Many of the books of the New Testament are actually letters. Paul, one of the first missionaries, wrote many of the letters. In his letters, Paul explained about what it meant to be a follower of Christ. He gave the people instructions and encouragement. Listen to this verse. It's** from a letter Paul wrote to people who lived in Thessalonica. Read 1 Thessalonians 5:11. Then write the verse on the chalkboard or newsprint, and have the children read it with you. Ask:

● **In what ways do you give and receive encouragement from other Christians?**

● **Why do you think Paul gave this instruction to the people of Thessalonica?**

● **What words of encouragement do you think would be helpful for you to give to other Christians?**

Say: **Let's take a moment to encourage each other.** Have each child say something encouraging to the person on his or her left, such as, "Thanks for showing your love for God by being a good friend." After each child shares, have the entire class recite the verse.

Say: **It's good to encourage each other. Now let's offer encouragement to Christians from another church. We're going to write letters to children your age from another church. In your letter, introduce yourself and explain what we've been learning in class. Be sure to include some encouraging words to help these other children live for Jesus.**

Tell the children what church they will be writing to and where it is located. If you have any background information on the church or the location, give that to the children as well.

Pass out the paper, markers or pens, and stickers. Tell the children to begin their letters with, "Dear Christian friend." When the letters are written, have children write the Bible verse and then sign their names. Finally, they can decorate their letters with stickers and drawings.

When the children are finished, read the cover letter you have written; then collect the children's letters and place them in the envelope. You may also want to include a copy of your church bulletin or newsletter, and a drawing or photograph of your church. As the children watch, address the envelope, and let one of them seal it. Chose another child to write the verse on the back of the envelope. When this is done, ask each child to help decorate the back of the envelope with more stickers.

Have the children gather round and pile their hands on top of the letter. Pray: **Dear God, Just as Paul did years ago, we are sending out letters to Christians at another church. We ask that our words might encourage our Christian friends to live lives that are pleasing to you. Amen.**

Your children may receive a reply to the letters. Your group may want to continue to correspond with the children of the other church. Consider sending them a tape of your group singing, a video production, self-portraits and other works of art, holiday greetings, prayers the children write, photographs, and/or handmade bookmarks.

✛ REFLECTIVE

Good Habits

> *"Be joyful always; pray continually; give thanks in all circumstances, for this is God's will for you in Christ Jesus."*
>
> 1 THESSALONIANS 5:16-18

SUPPLIES: You'll need a Bible, a chalkboard and chalk or newsprint and a marker, paper, and pencils. You may also want to provide some quiet, reflective music for the children to listen to.

Hand out paper and pencils. Say: **I'd like you to think about yourself for a few minutes and write down a list of everything about yourself that will always be true. For example, you could write down that your eyes will always be blue, but you couldn't write down that your hair will always be black because chances are someday your hair will turn gray. Think about physical characteristics and also think about what you do, what you think about, how you feel and your relationships with others.**

Give the children a couple of minutes to write their lists. Then have the children share their lists with a partner. Say: **There's a verse in the Bible that talks about some attitudes that God wants us to always have. Let's read the verse.**

Look up 1 Thessalonians 5:16-18, read it aloud, and write in it on the chalkboard or newsprint. Then have the children recite the verse by reading it aloud phrase by phrase and having the children repeat after you. Ask:

● **How are the qualities of this verse similar to or different from the things you put on your list?**

● **What do you think about this verse? Is it possible for us to always be joyful? to pray continually? to give thanks in all circumstances?**

Say: **It's tough to understand this verse. It's hard to know how to be joyful always—even when your dog dies. It's hard to know how to pray continually when you've got to do your homework sometime. And it's hard to give thanks in all circumstances including that time when the bully on bus made fun of you. But since these things are written in Scripture, they are commands that Christians are expected to obey. That means that there must be some way to really do these things.**

We're going to take several minutes to think about this verse and consider how these commands are possible. Write down the verse on your papers,

and then create three sections on your paper. Write down your ideas about how you can do this verse. You can draw pictures, doodles, stories, fables, or anything else that will help you explore how you can follow this verse.

Give the children several minutes to think and write. Periodically get their attention and say: **Let's say the verse together to help us refocus our attention.** Each time you do this, use a different voice or emphasis to help the children consider the verse in a new way. For example, you might use a questioning voice, a whispering voice, an emphatic voice, or a shouting voice. You may also want to play quiet music while the children are thinking.

Be ready to help children who can't make sense out of the verse. You might explain that it's possible to have joy even when circumstances are dismal because of God's love, that it's possible to have a prayerful spirit that's always ready to listen to God no matter what you're doing, or that it's possible to be thankful for the lessons we learn in the midst of trials.

After several minutes, have volunteers share their ideas. Then say: **We know that God's Word is always true. You've had deep insights into how this verse can be true. Let's say the verse one more time. This time, we'll let the tone of our voices show that we firmly believe these statements are true and that we intend to follow these commands.** Repeat the verse one last time with the children.

VISUAL-SPATIAL

Breathed by God

> *"All Scripture is God-breathed and is useful for teaching, rebuking, correcting and training in righteousness, so that the man of God may be thoroughly equipped for every good work."*
>
> 2 TIMOTHY 3:16-17

SUPPLIES: You'll need a Bible, newsprint, tape, a dictionary, a fan, streamers or Christmas tree tinsel, a chalkboard and chalk, and markers.

Tape newsprint to the wall to create a mural. Make sure the mural is big enough for all of the children to have room to draw. Put a bucket of markers near the mural paper. Write the memory verse on the chalkboard or newsprint.

Gather the children and read the verse aloud with them. Say: **In some versions of the Bible, the term "God-breathed" is translated as "inspired." Think for a moment about the word picture that comes to your mind when you hear the word "God-breathed."** Ask:

● **What do the words "inspired" and "God-breathed" mean to you?**

● **What do these words tell you about the Bible?**

Say: **Now let's talk about what the Bible is used for. The verse uses four terms: teaching, rebuking, correcting, and training in righteousness.** Ask:

● **What do these terms mean?**

Allow the children to use a dictionary to look up unfamiliar terms. Ask:

● **The last phrase of the verse explains what the purpose of Scripture is—the end result of Scripture's rebuking, correcting and training. What is that end result?**

● **How do the words of Scripture equip—help or prepare—people to do good works?**

Say: **I've brought in some props to help us create a visual picture of this verse. I have a fan and some streamers. Let's tape the streamers to the fan. For each streamer we tape on, let's say the verse together and mention something from Scripture that rebukes us, corrects us, trains us or equips us for good works.**

Give each child a streamer. As each child tapes his or her streamer to the fan, have the class recite the verse. Then have a volunteer suggest something from Scripture that rebukes, corrects, trains, or equips. For example, someone might mention one of the Ten Commandments or one of the fruits of the Spirit.

Then say: **Now I'll plug in the fan. Watch the streamers blow in the breeze of the fan, and imagine it's God breathing the words of Scripture. Then think of how Scripture rebukes, corrects, trains and equips. Draw a picture on the mural paper of how God's Word does one of these four things.**

Set up the fan so that it blows toward the mural. Make sure that none of the children approach the fan while it's turned on. Have the children draw pictures on the mural.

After several minutes. turn off the fan and have the children explain what they've drawn. Then say the verse aloud one more time.

 **interpersonal**

Encouragement Gauntlet

> *"And let us consider how we may spur one another on toward love and good deeds."*
>
> **HEBREWS 10:24**

SUPPLIES: You'll need a Bible.

Gather the children together. Say: **At one time or another, all of us have done a good deed for someone else. Take a moment to think of a good deed that you've done that you can share with the rest of us.** Give the children a moment to think of ideas. Then have volunteers share their good deeds with the rest of the class.

Say: **Your good deeds are wonderful, but sometimes we need a bit of encouragement to keep on doing good deeds.**

Have a volunteer read Hebrews 10:24. Say: **There's a word in that verse that we don't use very much. It's the word "spur."** Ask:

● **In what context have you heard the word "spur"?**

● **What do you think it means to "spur one another on toward love and good deeds"?**

● **Why is it important for Christians to do this for each other?**

Say: **This verse tells us to consider how to get others to do good. Let's do some considering right now.** Ask:

● **What practical things can we do to spur one another on?**

● **How could we use words to encourage each other?**

Say: **It's important for us to practice what we read in Scripture. Let's practice this verse.**

Form two groups. Have the groups stand in two lines facing each other with about three feet between them. This will form a "gauntlet."

Say: **To do this activity, we'll take turns walking slowly between the two groups. As one person walks, the rest of us will say things to spur him or her on toward love and good deeds. We'll say those encouraging words as the person walks past us. And we'll each put a hand on his or her back or shoulder. Push gently until you can't reach him or her anymore. We want each person to hear the encouragement of our words and to feel the encouragement of our touch, spurring him or her on.**

When the person reaches the end of the gauntlet, we'll all say the verse together. Ready? Here we go.

Repeat the activity for each child. As the children emerge at the end of the gauntlet, have them join one of lines so that they can encourage the next person who comes through. Be sure to recite the verse after each child goes through the gauntlet.

When everyone has traveled through the gauntlet, pray: **Dear God, we pray that we will remember the encouragement and advice our friends have just given us. May it spur us on toward love and good deeds! Amen.**

Logical-Mathematical

Faith of Our Fathers

> *"Remember your leaders, who spoke the word of God to you. Consider the outcome of their way of life and imitate their faith."*
>
> HEBREWS 13:7

SUPPLIES: You'll need a Bible, a chalkboard and chalk or newsprint and a marker, paper, and pencils.

Write out the verse at the very top of the chalkboard or newsprint, leaving plenty of room underneath. Lead children in reading the verse aloud.

Say: **Today we're going to follow the advice of this verse. The first thing this verse tells us to do is to "remember your leaders who spoke the word of God to you."** Have the children repeat the sentence. Then say: **The first thing I want you to do is to remember your Christian leaders. Write a list of all the Christian leaders you can think of.**

Hand out paper and pencils, and have the children write a vertical list of at least four or five Christian leaders, such as the pastors in your church, older people in your church, parents, and even famous or historical people such as Billy Graham or Martin Luther. Make sure the children leave plenty of room between the names on their lists.

Give the children a few minutes, then say: **The next thing this verse tells us to do is to "consider the outcome of their way of life."** Have the children repeat the sentence. Then ask:

● **What do you think this means?**

Say: **Let's think about how these people have lived their Christian lives. What kinds of things do they do to show they're strong Christians? How have those actions affected their lives? Write down your ideas next to each person's name on your list.**

Give the children several minutes. Then say: **Last, this verse tells us to "imitate their faith." Make a third column on your paper, and write what you've learned about being a Christian from each person and how you can follow his or her example.**

Give the children a few minutes. Then have volunteers share what they've written. Copy what they say onto the chalkboard under the appropriate phrase of the verse. After each person is mentioned, have the children read aloud the verse, while you point to the appropriate examples from the children's lists. For example, Troy might give the example of his Uncle Bill who never uses bad words even when he's mad. Troy decided to guard his tongue and his temper. While the children all say, "Remember your leaders who spoke the word of God to you," you'll point to the words "Uncle Bill." While the children say, "consider the outcome of their way of life," you'll point to the words, "never uses bad words." And when the children say "and imitate their faith," you'll point to the words, "Troy will guard his tongue and temper."

Continue this activity for each volunteer who wants to share from his or her list.

InterPersonal

Where to Share?

> *"And do not forget to do good and to share with others, for with such sacrifices God is pleased."*
>
> HEBREWS 13:16

SUPPLIES: You'll need a Bible, a chalkboard and chalk or newsprint and a marker, and enough individually wrapped candy for each child to have five pieces.

Write the verse on a chalkboard or newsprint for children to use as a reference.

Say: **Today we're going to act out Hebrews 13:16: "And do not forget** to do good and to share with others, for with such sacrifices God is pleased." I'm going to give you five pieces of candy. Your job will be to give away all five pieces of candy one piece at a time to five different people. Keep giving away candy until you don't have any left. But remember that while you are giving away candy, all your other classmates will also be giving away candy. You must graciously accept the candy they give you and give it away to someone else. Ready? Here we go.

Play the game for three or four minutes. The children will discover that as fast as they give candy away, they get more candy. Call time and have the children sit with a partner to discuss these questions:

- **What did you like the best about this game?**
- **How did it feel to share what you had with others in the class?**
- **What happened when you shared?**
- **What happens in real life when you do good and share with others?**

Call the group back together, and have the children share the good answers their partners gave for the questions. Then say: **The last part of this verse says "with such sacrifices God is pleased."** Ask:

- **In what ways is it a sacrifice to do good and to share?**
- **Did you feel like you were sacrificing in our game? Why or why not?**
- **Did you end up with the same amount of candy that you started with?**
- **How is this similar to or different than real life?**

Say: **In our lives, we don't have any guarantee that we'll receive anything in return when we give to others. Things don't always turn out equal, but we can know that God is pleased when we share what we have with others. Get with your partner again, and think of some things you could give to others. When one partner mentions an idea, the other partner will respond by saying the verse. Then switch roles. Continue until each of you has mentioned at least five different things.**

Have the partners share their ideas and repeat the verse until each partner has shared at least five ideas. End the activity by having the children share their ideas with the entire class.

Pure Joy

> *"Consider it pure joy, my brothers, whenever you face trials of many kinds, because you know that the testing of your faith develops perseverance."*
>
> JAMES 1:2-3

SUPPLIES: You'll need a Bible and a chalkboard and chalk or newsprint and a marker.

Say: **Today we're going to look at a Bible verse that tells us what to do when we go through trials.** Ask:

● **What is a trial?**

Say: **A trial might be defined as a tough time that you're going through or some kind of trouble. At one time or another, all of us undergo trials. For example, maybe your favorite uncle is in the hospital and you're worried, or you're having a tough time understanding a new concept in math, or maybe you're fighting with your best friend. Let's see what the Bible tells us to do when we face trials.**

Look up and read aloud James 1:2-3. Have the children say it with you. You may want to write it on a chalkboard or newsprint so the children can refer to the verse throughout the activity.

Say: **This verse says that we should have joy when we face trials because trials help us to develop perseverance.** Ask:

● **What is perseverance?**

Say: **One definition of perseverance is stick-to-it-iveness. When we persevere, we don't give up—we stick with it. Let's say the verse again.** Repeat the verse with the children. Ask:

● **Why is it important to persevere?**

Say: **Let's consider some logical outcomes that will come when we persevere during trials and troubles. First let's brainstorm about some trials and troubles.**

Have the children think of trials and troubles. List their answers on the chalkboard. Then say: **I'll put the word "perseverance" in the middle of the chalkboard because no matter what the trial is, according to this verse, God wants us use the trial to develop perseverance.** Write the word "perseverance" in the middle of chalkboard. Then say: **Now let's consider what perseverance**

will do for us when we go through each of these specific trials.

Discuss each of the trials the children mentioned using this procedure:

● recite the verse together,

● read the trial aloud, and

● discuss what good things will result from persevering through the trial.

For example, in persevering through a fight with a best friend, a child might deepen the friendship or learn how to resolve conflict.

Continue through the entire list of trials. Then say: **This Scripture passage goes on to say what the overall reward to developing perseverance is.** Read James 1:2-4. Then say: **God's Word says that when we develop perseverance, we're on the way to being mature and complete. We really can consider trials joyfully because God is using trials to help us grow into mature, complete Christians.**

🎵 MUSICAL

Harmonic Living

> *"Finally, all of you, live in harmony with one another, be sympathetic, love as brothers. Be compassionate and humble."*
>
> **1 PETER 3:8**

SUPPLIES: You'll need a Bible, newsprint, and a marker.

Teach your children this song to help them learn 1 Peter 3:8. Write the words on a sheet of newsprint as they appear below. Sing the words to the tune of "Three Blind Mice." The words don't fit exactly into the tune. Challenge your musical learners to make the words fit without changing them.

Finally, finally,
All of you, all of you,
Live in harmony with one another,
Be sympathetic, love as brothers.
Be compassionate and humble.
1 Peter 3:8.
1 Peter 3:8.

Once the children are comfortable with the song, divide the group into three smaller groups, and have them sing the song as a round. If your children are inexperienced round singers, have the three groups stand separate from each other. But if your children are experienced singers, have the children mix up the groups to sing the round—this way, they'll hear the harmonies better. After you've sung the round several times, ask:

- **What do you like about singing in harmony?**
- **What's tricky or hard about singing in harmony?**
- **How is singing in harmony like living in harmony?**
- **What can you do to be sympathetic, compassionate, and humble?**

Have the children write additional verses to the song that tell ways to be sympathetic, compassionate, and humble.

LinGuistiC

Wolves and Other Dangerous Lies

> *"For, whoever would love life and see good days must keep his tongue from evil and his lips from deceitful speech."*
>
> **1 PETER 3:10**

SUPPLIES: You will need Bibles, paper, and pencils.

Say: **Fables are stories that have a "moral." They help people remember an important lesson for living.** Ask:

- **If I said to you, "Slow and steady wins the race," what story would I be talking about?**

Say: **Here's another example of a fable. We all know the story of "The Boy Who Cried Wolf."** Ask:

- **What important lesson does this story teach?**

Say: **There's a Bible verse that could be used as a moral for that story. It's 1 Peter 3:10: "For, whoever would love life and see good days must keep his tongue from evil and his lips from deceitful speech."**

We are going to form groups to come up with new stories that could

If your group is more reflective than social, you may want to have the children write their own stories instead of developing stories and skits in groups. Give the children ten minutes to write their stories. Then have them read the stories. After each story, have the child say, "And the moral of the story is…" and have the class join together in saying the Bible verse and reference.

use the same verse as a moral. Your story needs to include someone who either lies or is tempted to lie. And your story can either show the trouble the person gets into because of the lie, or it can show the reward the person receives for being truthful.

Be ready to act out your story for the rest of us. Make sure that each person in your group has a role. Your story should last no longer than three minutes.

Have the kids form groups of three. Hand out paper and pencils. Give the groups about ten minutes to create their stories and practice acting it out. Watch the groups carefully. Be ready to appoint a director or help resolve conflict if necessary.

After each group has developed its own story, watch the skits. After each story is presented, cue the audience using the words, "And the moral of the story is…" At this point, the whole group will join together in repeating the Bible verse and reference.

LOGICAL-MATHEMATICAL

Teeter-Totter Humility

> "Humble yourselves, therefore, under God's mighty hand, that he may lift you up in due time."
>
> 1 PETER 5:6

SUPPLIES: You'll need a narrow board (2x4) about five feet long, a fulcrum (triangular piece of wood to place under the board), two small boxes, a glove, a weight to put in the glove (such as a rock), index cards or pieces of paper, and pens.

To prepare for this activity, place the board on the fulcrum, and put one box on each side of the board. This will create a "scale" to measure humility. Have the scale slightly "off" so one side falls down. Put the weight in the glove. Then give each child four index cards and a pen.

Read the verse, and have the class say it together. Ask for some examples or definitions of humility. Say: **This verse tells us that if we humble ourselves,**

God will lift us up. Write down on each card a way that you can show humility, or a way that would not show humility.

After the class has had time to write, ask for a volunteer to read one card. Then ask the class:

● **Do you think that this is an example of humility, or not?**

After the class responds, have the child place the card in the box on the side that is "down." Then if the card was an example of humility, have the child place the weighted glove in the other box. Watch "God's hand" lift up the other box. If the card was not an example of humility, don't place the glove in the box. Next have the class say the verse together, with the reference.

Allow all the children to read their cards and determine whether they've written examples of humility or not. Repeat the verse each time.

After each child has had a turn, ask:

● **Why does God want us to humble ourselves?**

● **Why do you think God promises to lift up those who humble themselves?**

● **In what ways will God lift up those who humble themselves?**

Say: **God wants us to recognize that we are his children. When we humble ourselves, we put ourselves under God's leadership and we put ourselves in a position to serve others. God promises to reward us for following him and serving others. God promises to lift us up.**

♩♪ MUSICAL

Clinking Cares

> *"Cast all your anxiety on him because he cares for you."*
>
> **1 PETER 5:7**

SUPPLIES: You'll need a Bible; a large metal mixing bowl; a dish towel; pens; masking tape; and an assortment of metal objects such as pliers, wrenches, screwdrivers, assorted screws, silverware, and serving utensils. You'll need at least one metal item for each child.

This activity works especially well in a small room. If your room is large, gather the children in a small circle for this activity so that the noise is loud and bothersome.

Put the metal objects in the mixing bowl, and set it where children can see it. Pick up a handful of the metal objects and drop them into the bowl. Do this several times and observe children's reaction to the clatter. Ask:

● **Can you imagine what it would be like to listen to that sound all day long?**

● **How would that make you feel?**

● **How is that like or unlike the way you feel when you're anxious or worried about something?**

Have the children form pairs. Say: **Choose an object from the bowl to represent your anxieties, and tell your partner why you chose it. For example, you might choose a fork because it seems like your worries are always poking at you. Choose an object now.**

Help kids choose their objects and find partners. Allow a few minutes for partners to describe their anxiety objects, and then call kids back together. Say: **Now tell your partner at least one thing that makes you worried. Write your anxiety on a piece of masking tape, and tape it to your metal object. If you have more than one anxiety, you may choose another object.**

After kids have taped their anxieties to their objects, gather everyone back together. Say: **Let's talk about our worries. As you mention your anxiety, drop your object into the metal bowl.**

When all of the children have dropped their anxieties into the bowl. Say: **Worries grate on us: They bother us and make us uneasy.** Hold up the dish towel. **But God's Word says that God cares about our worries.** Open a Bible and read 1 Peter 5:7. **The Bible says that God can take care of all our anxieties.**

It says to cast or throw our cares onto God. Let's add this dish towel to the bowl and see what happens when we throw our cares on God.

Empty the bowl and distribute the anxiety objects again. Line the bowl with the thick cloth and say: **Now let's cast our anxieties on God. As we say our memory verse, drop your metal object into the bowl.**

As you say each word of the verse, have one child drop his or her object into the bowl. The sounds will be muffled because of the dish towel. Repeat the verse until all the objects are back in the bowl. Ask:

● **How did the dish towel change this activity?**

● **In what ways does God take care of our anxieties?**

Say: **Let's thank God for his care.**

Pray: **God, we thank you for being a God who cares for us. You take care of us every day. We praise you for loving us enough to take all of our cares and anxieties away. Amen.**

 MUSICAL

Forgiveness Feelings

> *"If we confess our sins, he is faithful and just and will forgive us our sins and purify us from all unrighteousness."*
>
> 1 JOHN 1:9

SUPPLIES: You'll need a Bible, a CD or cassette player, and several recordings of happy and sad instrumental music. You might gather a collection of popular, sad ballads, jazzy praise tunes, and light classical music. Include selections in both major and minor keys. Often the title of a classical piece will tell you what the key signature is. Selections in minor keys are often titled as this example: "Vivaldi's Concerto in A minor for violin." Selections in major keys will often simply list the key—for example, "Bach's Concerto in E for violin."

pen your Bible to 1 John 1:9, read the verse aloud, and have children repeat it with you. Ask:

● **How do you feel when you know you've sinned?**

Let children respond; then say: **Sin makes us feel bad inside. We're** going to listen to several music selections. When you hear music that sounds like the way you feel when you've sinned, raise your hand.

Play several music selections including at least one that in a happy or major key. Let children respond by raising their hands. Invite them to explain why they chose the music they did. Have the children vote to choose which music they think best represents the feeling of sin.

After you've chosen a selection, ask:

● **How do you feel when someone forgives you for something you've done?**

Let children respond, then say: **Forgiveness makes us feel good inside—and God's forgiveness makes us feel really good. When we confess our sin and receive God's forgiveness, it's as if our sin never happened. I'm going to play some more music now. When you hear music that sounds like the way you feel when you've been forgiven, raise your hand.** Play several music selections including at least one in a sad or minor key. Let children choose one selection that best represents the feeling of forgiveness.

Have kids spread out around the room. Say: **We're going to use our music selections during a prayer time now. We'll say our verse together; then I'll play our sinful feeling music while we silently confess our sins to God. When the music stops we'll say the verse again. Then I'll play our forgiveness feeling music and we can silently thank God for his forgiveness.**

Lead children in repeating the verse, and then play the music for prayers of confession. Repeat the verse again, and then play the music for prayers of thanksgiving for forgiveness. When the music stops, close in prayer.

✹ Logical-Mathematical

Living in Love

> *"God is love. Whoever lives in love lives in God, and God in him."*
>
> 1 John 4:16b

SUPPLIES: You'll need a chalkboard and chalk or dry-erase board and a marker, paper, and pens.

Read the verse aloud, and then repeat it together with the class. Give each child a piece of paper and pen. Then have the children each draw a large heart on their papers.

Say: **This verse teaches us about being loving. It says that if we live in love, we will live in God.** Ask:

● **How do we live in love?**

Say: **Inside the heart, write several things you do that are loving. In addition, write down some things that God has done that are loving. Then, outside the heart, write several things that are not loving.**

While the children are writing, draw a large heart on the chalkboard or dry-erase board. After the children have had time to write, ask for volunteers to read one of the actions they've written down. Say to the class: **If you think the phrase is something loving that God has done, then say, "God is love." If you think the phrase is something that** (name) **does that is loving, say, "Whoever lives in love lives in God, and God in him." And if you think the phrase is something not loving, say, "That's not love."**

Have the volunteer read one action, let the children categorize it; then write the phrase on the chalkboard either inside the heart (if it is loving) or outside the heart (if it is not loving).

Continue to write the phrases on the board, either inside the heart or outside the heart.

Then repeat the entire verse together with the children.

Indexes

SCRIPTURE INDEX

AGE-LEVEL INDEX

Multiple Intelligence Index

Group Publishing, Inc.
Attention: Product Development
P.O. Box 481
Loveland, CO 80539
Fax: (970) 669-1994

Evaluation for *Making Scripture Memory Fun*

Please help Group Publishing, Inc., continue to provide innovative and useful resources for ministry. Please take a moment to fill out this evaluation and mail or fax it to us. Thanks!

● ● ●

1. As a whole, this book has been (circle one)

not very helpful   very helpful
1   2   3   4   5   6   7   8   9   10

2. The best things about this book:

3. Ways this book could be improved:

4. Things I will change because of this book:

5. Other books I'd like to see Group publish in the future:

6. Would you be interested in field-testing future Group products and giving us your feedback? If so, please fill in the information below:

Name _____

Street Address _____

City _____ State _____ Zip _____

Phone Number _____ Date _____

Exciting Resources for Your Adult Ministry

Sermon-Booster Dramas

Tim Kurth

Now you can deliver powerful messages in fresh, new ways. Set up your message with memorable, easy-to-produce dramas—each just 3 minutes or less! These 25 low-prep dramas hit hot topics ranging from burnout...ethics...parenting...stress...to work...career issues and more! Your listeners will be on the edge of their seats!

ISBN 0-7644-2016-X

Fun Friend-Making Activities for Adult Groups

Karen Dockrey

More than 50 relational programming ideas help even shy adults talk with others at church! You'll find low-risk Icebreakers to get adults introduced and talking... Camaraderie-Builders that help adults connect and start talking about what's really happening in their lives...and Friend-Makers to cement friendships with authentic sharing and accountability.

ISBN 0-7644-2011-9

Bore No More
(For Every Pastor, Speaker, Teacher)

Mike & Amy Nappa

This is a must-have for pastors, college/career speakers, and others who address groups! Because rather than just provide illustrations to entertain audiences, the authors show readers how to involve audiences in the learning process. The 70 sermon ideas presented are based on New Testament passages, but the principles apply to all passages.

ISBN 1-55945-266-8

Young Adult Faith-Launchers

These 18 in-depth Bible studies are perfect for young adults who want to strengthen their faith and deepen their relationships. They will explore real-world issues...ask the tough questions...and along the way turn casual relationships into supportive, caring friendships. Quick prep and high involvement make these the ideal studies for peer-led Bible studies, small groups, and classes.

ISBN 0-7644-2037-2

More Resources for Your Children's Ministry

Quick Children's Sermons: Will My Dog Be in Heaven?

Kids ask the most amazing questions—and now you'll be ready to answer 50 of them! You'll get witty, wise, and biblically solid answers to kid-size questions...and each question and answer makes a wonderful children's sermon. This is an attention-grabbing resource for children's pastors, Sunday school teachers, church workers, and parents.

ISBN 1-55945-612-4

"Let's Play!" Group Games for Preschoolers

Make playtime learning time with great games that work in any size class! Here are more than 140 easy-to-lead, fun-to-play games that teach preschoolers about Bible characters and stories. You'll love the clear, simple directions, and your kids will love that they can actually do these games!

ISBN 1-55945-613-2

More Than Mud Pies

Preschoolers love making crafts...but finished crafts are often forgotten long before the glue dries. Until now! These 48 3-D crafts become fun games your preschoolers will play again and again. And every time they play, your preschoolers will be reminded of important Bible truths. Each craft comes with photocopiable game instructions to send home to parents!

ISBN 0-7644-2044-5

The Discipline Guide for Children's Ministry

Jody Capehart, Gordon West & Becki West

With this book you'll understand and implement classroom-management techniques that work—and that make teaching fun again! From a thorough explanation of age-appropriate concerns...to proven strategies for heading off discipline problems before they occur...here's a practical book you'll turn to again and again!

ISBN 1-55945-686-8

Order today from your local Christian bookstore, or write: Group Publishing, P.O. Box 485, Loveland, CO 80539.

Group's hands-On BiBLE curriculum™

TEACH YOUR PRESCHOOLERS AS JESUS TAUGHT WITH GROUP'S *HANDS-ON BIBLE CURRICULUM*™

Hands-On Bible Curriculum™ **for preschoolers** helps your preschoolers learn the way they learn best—by touching, exploring, and discovering. With active learning, preschoolers love learning about the Bible, and they really remember what they learn.

Because small children learn best through repetition, Preschoolers and Pre-K & K will learn one important point per lesson, and Toddlers & 2s will learn one point each month with **Hands-On Bible Curriculum**. These important lessons will stick with them and comfort them during their daily lives. Your children will learn:

- God is our friend,
- who Jesus is, and
- we can always trust Jesus.

The **Learning Lab**® is packed with age-appropriate learning tools for fun, faith-building lessons. Toddlers & 2s explore big **Interactive StoryBoards**™ with enticing textures that toddlers love to touch—like sandpaper for earth, cotton for clouds, and blue cellophane for water. While they hear the Bible story, children also *touch* the Bible story. And they learn. **Bible Big Books**™ captivate Preschoolers and Pre-K & K while teaching them important Bible lessons. With **Jumbo Bible Puzzles**™ and involving **Learning Mats**™, your children will see, touch, and explore their Bible stories. Each quarter there's a brand-new collection of supplies to keep your lessons fresh and involving.

Fuzzy, age-appropriate hand puppets are also available to add to the learning experience. What better way to teach your class than with the help of an attention-getting teaching assistant? These child-friendly puppets help you teach each lesson with scripts provided in the **Teacher Guide**. Plus, your children will enjoy teaching the puppets what they learn. Cuddles the Lamb, Whiskers the Mouse, and Pockets the Kangaroo turn each lesson into an interactive and entertaining learning experience.

Just order one **Learning Lab** and one **Teacher Guide** for each age level, add a few common classroom supplies, and presto—you have everything you need to inspire and build faith in your children. For more interactive fun, introduce your children to the age-appropriate puppet who will be your teaching assistant and their friend. No student books are required!

Hands-On Bible Curriculum is also available for elementary grades.

Order today from your local Christian bookstore, or write: Group Publishing, P.O. Box 485, Loveland, CO 80539.